The Customer-Driven Playbook

Converting Customer Feedback into Successful Products

Travis Lowdermilk and Jessica Rich

Beijing · Boston · Farnham · Sebastopol · Tokyo

The Customer-Driven Playbook

by Travis Lowdermilk and Jessica Rich

Published by O'Reilly Media, Inc., 1005 Gravenstein
Highway North, Sebastopol, CA 95472.

O'Reilly books may be purchased for educational, business, or sales
promotional use. Online editions are also available for most titles
(*https://oreilly.com/safari*). For more information, contact our corporate/
institutional sales department: 800-998-9938 or *corporate@oreilly.com*.

Development Editor: Angela Rufino

Acquisitions Editor: Mary Treseler

Production Editor: Colleen Cole

Copyeditor: Rachel Monaghan

Proofreader: Sonia Saruba

Indexer: Lucie Haskins

Interior Designer: David Futato

Cover Designer: Karen Montgomery

Illustrator: Rebecca Demarest

June 2017: First Edition

Revision History for the First Edition
2017-06-09: First Release

978-1-491-98127-6

[LSI]

This book belongs to Dr. Monty Hammontree, our team, and all our friends at Microsoft. Without them, this book would not have been possible.

[*contents*]

[*Preface*]

> "Over the next 10 weeks, we want you to come up with product ideas that can attract new customers and *triple* our revenue."

Susan, a UX lead for PartyTime Apps, felt her mouth fall open and heard the team shift uncomfortably in their chairs.

Susan and her team worked on an immensely popular mobile party-planning app called PartyOrganizr.

The app was at the top of the charts in all the mobile app stores, and the company had enjoyed several years of success. Yet leadership was looking for ways to capitalize on their success and generate new revenue.

They didn't have a lot of time, so Susan believed the team needed to be Lean. She was going to have the team talk to as many customers as they could, iterate quickly, and—above all else—"fail fast." She scheduled daily calls with customers and the team quickly fell into a cadence of meeting with customers, asking a myriad of questions, and taking copious notes.

The team had a lot of ideas about how they could generate new revenue, and they found that talking with customers was a great way to get direct feedback. Jerry, an engineer on the team, even started building a prototype for one of his ideas and began showing it to customers. It appeared that the team was on their way.

Then progress came to a complete halt. The team began arguing over what they were hearing from customers. Mary, a product manager, believed they weren't asking the right questions or talking to the right types of customers. Even though it would be costly to build, Jerry was convinced that customers liked his prototype. Richie, the team's software tester, became hyperfocused on fixing bugs that customers happened to mention on the calls. The team was divided and heading in separate directions.

After the 10 weeks was complete, the team was left with a half-baked prototype that leadership deemed a "solution in search of a problem." Even worse, after all the time they had spent with customers, the team had more questions than answers.

Does this sound familiar?

All too often, we find ourselves in this reality. While many Lean approaches and customer development strategies produced over the past decade have been transformational in how we think about building products, many teams find it difficult to put those principles into meaningful action.

That's why we've come up with *The Customer-Driven Playbook*. It's a complete end-to-end guide that will help you and your team move from understanding the customer to identifying their problems to conceptualizing new ideas—and ultimately to creating fantastic products.

Bottom line: this book will help you and your team put Lean theory into action.

Every element of this book has been used in the real world. This methodology has been proven successful in an organization of over 8,000 people that spans multiple countries.

Who Can Use the Customer-Driven Playbook?

Most of our experience in building this methodology has been in the software industry, so our book has been written primarily with software and technology products in mind. However, you can use our framework successfully when creating *any* product or service.

More specifically, this book is for program, product, project, or service managers; UX, visual, and interaction designers; UX researchers; team leads; engineers; testers; managers; and directors.

In short, if you have a desire to make great products, this book is for you.

How Is This Different from Other User-Centered Methodologies?

The customer-driven approach puts customers at the center. You may be asking, "How is that different from being *user*-centered?"

We believe a user and a customer have some subtle, yet profound, differences.

We call the people who use our products *customers* because it acknowledges the fact that they're *choosing* our products. When a customer chooses our product, it's an incredible gift and it's our responsibility to continually reward them for putting their trust in us.

Sam Walton was a multibillionaire who founded the colossal retail chains Walmart and Sam's Club. He once said:[1]

> There is only one boss. The customer. And he can fire everybody in the company, from the chairman on down, simply by spending his money somewhere else.

Walton knew that his customers had the power to dictate whether his business succeeded or failed. When you transform your thinking from *users* (people who are currently using your product) to *customers* (people who are choosing your product), it shows respect and appreciation for the people who are deciding to use your products.

The Customer-Driven Playbook approach goes beyond usability and usefulness. It considers the customer's motivation, goals, and desires, and starts to identify the problems and limitations that prevent them from achieving what they want to do.

Everyone is a customer—either a current customer, a potential customer, or a "churned" customer (someone who has recently abandoned your product). At any point, the customer may choose to join you or leave you. So, you must continually ask yourself:

> Who are my customers?
>
> What motivates them?
>
> What frustrates them or limits them from achieving their goals?
>
> What do they find valuable and useful?

And ultimately:

> How can I move customers from trying my products to needing them to loving them?

How This Book Is Organized

The foundation of this book, and our whole approach, is the *Hypothesis Progression Framework* (HPF). It has four stages: Customer, Problem, Concept, and Feature (see Figure P-1).

The HPF is the foundation that we'll use to successfully guide you through customer and product development.

The HPF is completely flexible. We've designed it so that it can work at whatever stage of development you're in. We've seen our framework scale to define new product categories, and we've seen it successfully revitalize existing products that have been available to customers for decades.

Additionally, we've organized the book to cover our *Customer-Driven Cadence* (see Figure P-2). These are three phases that you'll employ within each stage of the HPF (Formulating, Experimenting, and Sensemaking). This cadence has a familiar "build, measure, learn" (or "learn, build, measure") pattern that is found in many Lean approaches. You'll find that we repeat this pattern in all our playbooks.

Here's what we'll cover in each chapter:

Part I: The Foundation

Chapter 1: The Hypothesis Progression Framework and the Customer-Driven Cadence

> You'll learn about our foundational framework as well as our Customer-Driven Cadence. The framework and cadence will serve as an end-to-end guide to help you through customer and product development.

Chapter 2: Formulating

> You'll learn how to collect your assumptions and formulate them into hypotheses that can be tested. You'll also learn how to formulate a Discussion Guide, a set of questions that you can ask your customers to validate or invalidate your hypotheses.

Chapter 3: Experimenting

> You'll learn how to not only talk to customers, but find them as well. We'll also discuss the advantages and disadvantages of various research methods.

Chapter 4: Sensemaking

> While it's important to engage with customers and gather their feedback, the process is less impactful if you can't make sense out of the data you're collecting. In this chapter, you'll learn how to derive patterns and meaning in your data, and most importantly, share your findings throughout your organization.

Chapters 5, 6, 7, and 8 (Customer, Problem, Concept, and Feature)

> Through these chapters, we'll dive into each stage of the HPF. You'll learn the purpose of the stage and see examples of how hypotheses and structure can help the team. In the sidebars "PartyTime Apps Revisited," you'll get to follow along with our fictional-but-rooted-in-reality team, PartyTime Apps. You'll see how they use our methods to tackle the challenge presented earlier, achieving a much more successful outcome.

Chapter 9: Using the Playbooks

>This chapter gives a brief overview of how to use the play-books covered in Part II.

Part II: The Playbooks
Chapters 10, 11, 12, and 13

>We have a variety of design thinking activities and customer and product research methods that will help you track the progression of your assumptions, hypotheses, early ideas, concepts, and product features. Each stage of the Hypothesis Progression Framework has its own playbook and is placed in its own chapter so you can quickly find and reuse it.

Website

We have *a lot* of things we want to share. However, we're passionate about creating a book that's light, approachable, and engaging. We believe this book will be your companion guide to our approach. Our hope is that you'll find it continually useful and you'll return to it often as you begin to implement our framework and activities.

We've created a website (*customerdrivenplaybook.com*) that you can use alongside our book. This website will continue to grow, and it'll be the landing space for more in-depth activities, methodologies, cheat sheets, and approaches.

This book has everything you need to be successful. As you mature in your understanding, we encourage you to continually visit the website to learn new ways to leverage our framework.

O'Reilly Safari

Safari (formerly Safari Books Online) is a membership-based training and reference platform for enterprise, government, educators, and individuals.

Members have access to thousands of books, training videos, Learning Paths, interactive tutorials, and curated playlists from over 250 publishers, including O'Reilly Media, Harvard Business Review, Prentice Hall Professional, Addison-Wesley Professional, Microsoft Press, Sams, Que, Peachpit Press, Adobe, Focal Press, Cisco Press, John

Wiley & Sons, Syngress, Morgan Kaufmann, IBM Redbooks, Packt, Adobe Press, FT Press, Apress, Manning, New Riders, McGraw-Hill, Jones & Bartlett, and Course Technology, among others.

For more information, please visit *http://oreilly.com/safari*.

How to Contact Us

Please address comments and questions concerning this book to the publisher:

O'Reilly Media, Inc.
1005 Gravenstein Highway North
Sebastopol, CA 95472
800-998-9938 (in the United States or Canada)
707-829-0515 (international or local)
707-829-0104 (fax)

We have a web page for this book, where we list errata, examples, and any additional information. You can access this page at:

bit.ly/customer-driven-playbook

To comment or ask technical questions about this book, send email to:

bookquestions@oreilly.com

For more information about our books, courses, conferences, and news, see our website at *http://www.oreilly.com*.

Find us on Facebook: *http://facebook.com/oreilly*

Follow us on Twitter: *http://twitter.com/oreillymedia*

Watch us on YouTube: *http://www.youtube.com/oreillymedia*

Endnote

1   [anderson] p. 136

Part I

The Foundation

The Hypothesis Progression Framework and the Customer-Driven Cadence

In the summer of 2000, General Motors, an American car manufacturer, introduced the Pontiac Aztek, a radically new "crossover" vehicle—part sedan, part minivan, and part sports utility vehicle (see Figure 1-1). It was marketed as the do-it-all vehicle for 30-somethings. It was the car for people who enjoyed the outdoors, people with an "active lifestyle" and "none to one child."[1]

On paper, the Aztek appeared to be fully featured. It had a myriad of upgrades that included options for bike racks, a tent with an inflatable mattress, and an onboard air compressor. GM even included an option for an insulated cooler, to store beverages and cold items, between the passenger and driver seat. Their ideal customer was someone who would use the Aztek for everything from picking up groceries to camping out in the wilderness.

FIGURE 1-1
2001-2005
Pontiac Aztek

The Aztek had a polarizing visual aesthetic; many either loved or hated it (most hated it). Critics found its features, like the optional tent and cooler, awkward and downright gimmicky. GM insisted these were revolutionary ideas and suggested that they were ahead of their time. They believed that, once customers took the Aztek for a test drive, they would quickly realize just what they were missing.

After a $30 million marketing push,[2] it appeared that the critics were right. The Aztek failed to make even a modest dent in the overall market. The year that the Aztek was released, the American auto industry had sold 17.4 million vehicles. The Aztek represented only 11,000 of those vehicles (a number that some believed was still generously padded).[3]

To customers, the Aztek seemed to get in its own way. It was pushing an agenda by trying to convince customers how they *should* use their vehicles, rather than responding to how they *wanted* to use them.

It's easy to point at this example in hindsight and ask, "How could GM spend so much time, money, and resources only to produce a car no one wanted?" Some suggested it was because the car was "designed by committee" or that it was a good idea with poor execution.[4] Insiders blamed the "penny-pinchers" for insisting on cost-saving measures that ultimately produced a hampered product that wasn't at all consistent with the original vision.[5]

The lead designer of the Aztek, Tom Peters, went on to create many successful designs, like the C6 Chevy Corvette and 2014 Camaro Z/28, and eventually won a lifetime achievement award. He suggested that the poor design of the Aztek had started with the team asking themselves, "What would happen if we put a Camaro and an S10 truck in a blender?"[6]

The reality is that it was all of these reasons. Even though it appeared, at the time, that GM was "being innovative," they had forgotten the most crucial element: the customer. They had fallen in love with a concept and tried to find a customer who would want it.

They were running focus groups and also doing their own market research. They probably even created personas or some variant of the "ideal customer" that was perfect for the Aztek. GM believed they were being customer-focused. Yet they weren't paying attention to the right signals. They had respondents in focus groups saying, "Can they possibly be serious with this thing? I wouldn't take it as a gift!"[7]

While we can commend GM for trying to push the boundaries of the auto industry, we must admit that by not validating their assumptions and listening to their customers, they had created a solution in search of a problem.

We make assumptions about everything. It's a way for us to make meaning of what we understand based on our prior beliefs. However, our assumptions aren't always grounded in fact. They may come from "tribal knowledge," experience, or conventional wisdom. These sources start with a kernel of truth, which makes them *feel* real, but too often we mistake assumptions for facts.

This is not to say that assumptions are a bad thing. They can be incredibly useful in tapping into our intuition. It's when our assumptions go *unchecked* that we open ourselves to vulnerabilities in our design.

Unchecked assumptions can have a powerfully negative effect on our products, because they cause us to:

- Miss new opportunities or emerging market trends
- Make costly engineering mistakes by creating products that nobody will use
- Create technical debt by supporting features that customers aren't using
- Respond to problems too late

What's most dangerous about unchecked assumptions is that they become conventional wisdom and are carried so long that they create a false sense of security. Then a competitor swoops in with a better understanding of the customer and quickly takes over the entire market.

Henry Petroski, a professor at Duke University and expert in failure analysis, once said, "All conventional wisdom has an element of truth to it, but good design requires more than an element of truth—it requires an ensemble of correct assumptions and valid calculations."[8]

Therefore, it introduces a high level of risk if teams move forward with underlying assumptions that haven't been formulated, tested, and validated.

What Is the Hypothesis Progression Framework?

The Hypothesis Progression Framework (HPF) allows you to test your assumptions at any stage of the development process. At its heart, the HPF breaks up the development of products into four stages: Customer, Problem, Concept, and Feature (Figure 1-2).

FIGURE 1-2
The Hypothesis Progression Framework

Using the HPF, your team will:

- Formulate your assumptions into testable hypotheses
- Validate or invalidate your hypotheses by running experiments
- Make sense of what you've learned so that you can plan your next move

As the name suggests, the HPF is founded on the principle that if you state your assumptions as hypotheses and try to validate them, you will remain objective and focused on what the customer is telling you rather than supporting unconfirmed assumptions.

For now, understand that each stage in the HPF works together to address these fundamental questions (Figure 1-3):

Who are your customers?

When we sit down with teams, we will often hear something to the effect of, "Oh, we know who our customers are. That's not our problem." Then we'll ask questions like:

- What environments do your customers live/work in?
- Why do they choose *your* product over that of your competitors?
- What are they trying to achieve with your products?
- What unique attributes make your customers different from one another?

You may (or may not) be surprised how many teams have difficulty answering these types of questions.

Customer engagement is *not* customer development. It's one thing to engage customers by having an ongoing dialog using social networks, support forums, and the like. That's great. However, it's another thing entirely to systematically learn from your customers and generate actionable insights.

Your customers are not in a fixed position. Their values and tastes change over time. Therefore, you must be willing to journey with them and continually refine your products to remain one step ahead of where they plan to go.

What problems do they have?

At times, we get so enamored and focused on our solution that we need to step back and ask ourselves, "How many people are really experiencing this problem?" or "How much of a frustration is this problem for our customers?" If GM had been willing to ask their customers, "How valuable is it to have your car convert into a tent?" they would have learned that the tent was not solving a necessary problem for most of their customers. We must appreciate that, to create successful products, it's more than solving *a* problem—it's a matter of solving the *right* problem.

Will this concept solve their problem and do they find it valuable?

There are many ways to solve a problem, but how can you be confident you're solving it the right way? Are you sure that customers value the way you're trying to solve the problem, or are you introducing new problems you hadn't considered?

During the Concept stage, you're trying to ensure that you're solving the customer's problem in a way they find valuable.

You want to leverage your customers' feedback and continually validate that your ideas are on the right track. You'll establish the benefits of your concept (as well as its limitations) and increase your confidence that you're building something customers want.

Can they successfully use this feature and are they satisfied with it?

We've all been excited for a product release only to be disappointed later because it didn't deliver on its promises. Throughout the design and development process, you must ensure that your concept works as expected and is successful in helping customers solve their problems. While the Concept stage is to ensure you are building *the right thing*, the Feature stage ensures you are building it *the right way*.

FIGURE 1-3
The fundamental questions of the HPF

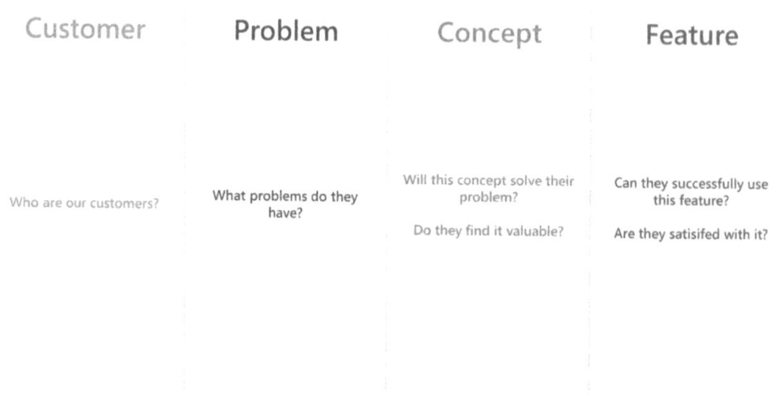

Customer	Problem	Concept	Feature
Who are our customers?	What problems do they have?	Will this concept solve their problem? Do they find it valuable?	Can they successfully use this feature? Are they satisfied with it?

By using the HPF as a guide, your team will remain customer-focused as it progresses through customer and product development. Together, these stages represent your entire solution. It's important to note that the HPF doesn't necessarily need be worked from left to right; it can be started at any stage. Depending on where you are in your product's development, you may decide to start at the Concept stage or Problem stage. However, you may start at a later stage in the HPF only to discover that you need to answer fundamental questions in the earlier stages. We've had teams come to us, ready to conduct usability testing on a feature, only to realize they didn't truly understand the customer or problem. That's what makes the HPF so profound: it allows teams to easily understand the stages that need to be validated to ship a successful product.

As we've discussed, your customers' needs evolve over time, and you must be willing to revisit your assumptions about your solution to ensure that it's meeting the right customer, solving the right problems, creating value, and making your customers successful.

The Customer-Driven Cadence

To remain Lean and customer-focused, teams must operate in a pattern of continuous learning and collaboration. The HPF has been designed to be used in parallel with your product development sprints or schedules. In short, you should be using the HPF while you're building and refining your products.

In Eric Ries's *Lean Startup* method, he calls for startups to engage in a "build, measure, learn" loop that accelerates learning and customer response.[9]

We've found tremendous success with this approach and have refined it to align more closely with our framework and activities in our playbooks. The Customer-Driven Cadence has three fundamental actions that you'll employ during each stage of the HPF: Formulating, Experimenting, and Sensemaking (Figure 1-4). Let's look at each of these individually:

Formulating (a.k.a. Build)

Throughout the entire customer-driven process, from customer to product development, you'll be formulating your assumptions, ideas, and hypotheses. This is an important practice because you will need to track the team's learning along the way. Ries refers to these key decision points as moments where a team needs to "pivot" (change direction) or "persevere" (continue the course).

By continually formulating your assumptions and stating them as hypotheses, your team will create a structure that allows you to easily track your assumptions about the customer, their problems, and your ideas of how to respond to those problems. Finally, you'll need to formulate a Discussion Guide. The Discussion Guide is the set of questions you'll ask customers in order to prove/disprove your assumptions.

Experimenting (a.k.a. Measure)

Each stage of the HPF has activities where you need to test whether your assumptions were correct. By continually running experiments against your hypotheses, you'll have the data you need to decide whether to pivot or persevere with your product's direction. While there are many methods you can employ to test your hypotheses, our book heavily emphasizes talking directly with customers.

Sensemaking (a.k.a. Learn)

The customer-driven approach relies on your ability to continually collect and make sense out of customer data. So often, teams fall into a cycle of "build, measure, build, measure, build, measure" and miss the overall learning or broad understanding of their customer. We've provided an activity in each of our playbooks that allows your team to pause and reflect on what you've all learned so that you can make informed decisions about where to go next.

FIGURE 1-4
The Customer-Driven
Cadence

	Customer	Problem	Concept	Feature
Build Formulating				
Measure Experimenting				
Learn Sensemaking				

Key Points

- Assumptions have a powerful effect on your product's outcome. When you follow unchecked assumptions about your customers, you run the risk of making mistakes, missing key business opportunities, or producing products that make little impact.

- Stating your assumptions as hypotheses allows you to remain objective and continually test what you believe to be true.

- The Hypothesis Progression Framework (HPF) is a structure that helps teams move between customer and product development. It consists of four stages: Customer, Problem, Concept, and Feature.

- Together, each stage of the HPF comprises your entire solution. The solution should be an ever-evolving response to your customers' needs.

- The Customer-Driven Cadence is a set of fundamental actions that you will employ during each stage of the HPF. With these actions, your team will fall into a pattern of formulating your ideas and assumptions into hypotheses, running experiments to validate them, and making sense out of your customer data.

Endnotes

1 [roca]
2 [miller], p. 26
3 [flint]
4 [atwood]
5 [weisman]
6 [seabaugh]
7 [lutz]
8 [petroski]
9 [ries]

[2]

Formulating

In the previous chapter, we discussed the powerfully negative effect that unchecked assumptions can have on our product decision-making. The best way to remain objective about your assumptions is to write hypotheses that can be tested with customer feedback.

Jeff Gothelf, coauthor of *Lean UX: Designing Great Products with Agile Teams*, sums it up perfectly:[1]

> Expressing your assumptions [using a hypothesis] turns out to be a really powerful technique. It takes much of the subjective and political conversation out of the decision-making process and instead orients the team toward feedback from the market. It also orients the team toward users and customers.

A Great Hypothesis Focuses on the Customer's Limitations, Not Your Own

Sometimes it can be difficult to separate our own internal or technical limitations from those of the customer. For example, we might believe that the lack of an effective search algorithm is causing customers to be frustrated.

We may construct a hypothesis that focuses on what *we* are lacking:

> We believe that, because our search algorithm produces ineffective results, customers are unwilling to create an account on our website.

This inwardly focused hypothesis already biases us toward one solution (adjust the search algorithm so it produces better results). It doesn't explore who the customer is, what they're trying to do, and how poor search results affect them.

This hypothesis is ineffective in its ability to help us gain greater insight about our customers. Are we sure that search results are the thing that's preventing customers from subscribing? If so, how effective do the search results need to be to get customers to purchase a subscription?

You may have heard the phrase "correlation is not causation." Be careful that you're not ascribing undesirable customer behavior to your own product's limitations. The two may be completely unrelated.

For example, you could invest a great deal of resources, increasing the speed and quality of search results, only to find that it had little effect on increasing subscriptions.

That's not to suggest that improving product quality is unimportant; however, we must continually ensure that quality of our product reflects what the customer wants to achieve with it. We shouldn't invest time and energy on things that have little customer impact. If spending months to shave a couple of milliseconds off your search results has no discernable impact on customer satisfaction, it may not be worth your investment.

Imagine this hypothesis instead:

> We believe that customers without an account prefer to see their results in order of closest to farthest from their location when searching for providers on our website.

This hypothesis connects the customer's motivation to one of our site's limitations. In other words, the customer wants to see results from closest to farthest, but we can't provide that functionality, because they don't have an account.

If we validated this hypothesis, we may decide that offering this functionality is of a high priority. Additionally, the specifics of this hypothesis help the engineering team understand what functionality we're looking to enable. It focuses their attention on one piece of functionality where we can improve search results (i.e., allowing customers to sort by location without having to log in to an account).

Formulating Assumptions into Hypotheses

In each of our playbooks, we give you an activity to help you collect your team's ideas or assumptions. Having a chance to "diverge" and get everything out there is a great way to see all the possible ideas and perspectives. We then like to "converge" by getting the teams to focus on a handful of possibilities presented. Typically, we do this by trying to find similarities or patterns in the group's thinking.

Throughout our individual playbooks, you'll find this continual "diverge" and "converge" pattern (Figure 2-1).

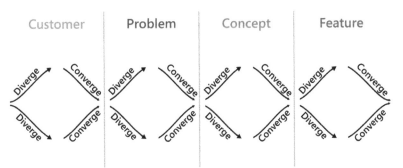

FIGURE 2-1
Throughout the HPF, you'll "diverge" (explore multiple assumptions and ideas) and "converge" (identify patterns and make decisions)

To help with formulating hypotheses, we provide our teams with a hypothesis template for each stage of the HPF (Figure 2-2). This helps them take their assumptions and formulate them into consistent hypotheses that can be tested. You can use these templates to help you get started, but the important thing to note isn't the syntax of the hypothesis, but rather the specific *parameters* we focus on at each stage. In short, you may need to alter the language of the hypothesis template to meet your needs, but we highly encourage you to keep the parameters.

Customer	Problem	Concept	Feature
[type of customers]			
[job-to-be-done]			
	[problem]		

FIGURE 2-2
The hypothesis templates of the HPF

Depending on where you are in your development cycle, you can choose to start at any stage in the HPF, but for now let's look at the hypothesis template for the Customer stage:

> We believe [type of customers] are motivated to [motivation] when doing [job-to-be-done].

We start each of our templates with the statement, "We believe." Some teams struggle with this because they might not have enough information to make a bold statement about what they believe. For example, if a team had been working on desktop software for over a decade and was suddenly tasked with creating a mobile app, they might feel uncomfortable making claims about what they believe mobile customers want.

These hypotheses templates shouldn't feel like legally binding contracts. It's a simple statement that illustrates what you believe given the information available to you. In the early stages of development, you might be operating with your gut instincts. That's perfectly okay, but it's better to capture those instincts so that you can appropriately validate them.

Most likely, your first hypotheses will be proven wrong. Therefore, you'll need to iterate them over time. It's a skill that can be sharpened, and you'll find that you'll get better at writing hypotheses the more you do it.

The Parameters of the Hypothesis Progression Framework

Each of our hypotheses templates has parameters that are highlighted at the stage they reside in. In the case of the Customer hypothesis, there are three parameters: [type of customers], [motivation], and [job-to-be-done]. These parameters will be carried throughout, helping inform the remaining stages. This is the *progression* of the Hypothesis Progression Model.

In Chapters 5 through 8, we cover each parameter in its respective stage, but there are three parameters that are shared throughout the HPF: [type of customers], [job-to-be-done], and [problem] (Figure 2-3). We call these the "shared parameters" because they create a common thread throughout the HPF. Let's look at them a bit more closely.

Customer Development		Product Development	
Customer	Problem	Concept	Feature
		We believe that [concept] will solve [problem] and be valuable to [type of customers] while doing [job-to-be-done]	We believe that [type of customers] will be successful solving [problem] using [feature] while doing [job-to-be-done]
We believe [type of customers] are motivated to [motivation] when doing [job-to-be-done]	We believe [type of customers] are frustrated by [job-to-be-done] because of [problem]	We will know this to be true when we see [criteria]	We will know they were successful when we see [criteria]

FIGURE 2-3
Shared parameters of the HPF

Type of Customers

Continually learning about your customers is paramount to the success of our framework. Throughout all stages we're interested in getting to know the specifics of the customer we're targeting. The Customer stage is where we define the customers we're targeting; however, it's important that we maintain the type of customer we're targeting to avoid confusion. For example, we might be looking at building an app for education. If our app would serve both students and teachers, it would be a mistake to talk to only students. There would be characteristics that differ between students and teachers, and it would be important to know what those are. By continually identifying and segmenting the customer you are talking about, you can ensure the team has a shared understanding of whom you're targeting (and whom you're not).

Job-to-Be-Done

The job-to-be-done parameter, based on Clayton Christensen's Jobs Theory, is the task the customer employs to reach their goal. Essentially, Christensen says that customers don't simply use products, they *hire* products to complete a job for them. Therefore, the Jobs Theory suggests that a job is *the progress that a person is trying to make in a particular circumstance.*[2]

For example, a customer doesn't want a drill, they want a quarter-inch hole. Therefore, they "hire" a drill to achieve that for them. Depending on the merits of the drill they choose, it will perform that job well or poorly.

We could write an entire book on just Jobs Theory alone, but there are plenty of them already out there. For now, all you need to know is that it's important to separate the job you're exploring from the motivation of your customer.

Imagine we work on a website portal that helps customers find local service providers in their area. Think of services like lawncare, childcare, housecleaning, and others.

Let's say we're interested in improving our customers' experience searching our website for local providers. We might ask our customers all sorts of questions, like how they use the search feature, what results they clicked on, or whether they use the site's advanced search tools. We might conclude that our customers' motivation is to "quickly find what they're looking for." However, this perspective is too general and lacks the specifics needed to make meaningful impact with the customer.

It's true that customers want fast search results, but it's the underlying motivations for those results that provide the insights we need to make innovative products.

For example, a customer comes to our site because he's motivated to find quality childcare. He could "hire" our search feature and quickly receive a list of providers in his area. However, we still didn't help him achieve his goal, because he's unable to sort the provider satisfaction rating from highest to lowest. Effectively, he has no easy way to discern which provider offers the highest-quality care.

In this example, if we separate the job-to-be-done (searching the site) from the motivation (finding quality childcare), we could track our product's performance against these parameters separately. This separation allows us to track multiple jobs as they relate to the customer's motivation. Our customer may have tried searching for a provider, but he might've also asked for recommendations on the member forum or read through provider reviews.

We'd want to know how each of these jobs performed in helping the customer achieve his goal.

Problem

If you're in the business of creating products, then you're in the business of solving problems. Therefore, it's important that you continually track the problem you're trying to solve and continually validate that problem with customers. This will help keep your development on track and away from feature or scope creep.

To effectively use the Hypothesis Progression Framework, it's important that you and your team become competent at writing hypotheses. Writing great hypotheses can be a bit of an art form, but with a little practice, you'll find that you're able to create them very quickly.

A great hypothesis:

- can be tested;
- reduces risk;
- is specific;
- separates the person from their behavior;
- focuses on the customer's limitations, not your own; and
- can be measured.

Let's review these principles a little more closely.

A GREAT HYPOTHESIS CAN BE TESTED

When you begin to test your assumptions with your customers, it's easy to fall into a false belief that, to "win," your assumptions must be proven right. This is an improper mindset for working and testing hypotheses. In fact:

> An invalidated hypothesis is just as valuable as a validated one.

We'll repeat this, in case you didn't read it the first time:

> An invalidated hypothesis is just as valuable as a validated one.

There are two *positive* outcomes for the results of a hypothesis. If you get results that align with what you expected, then your hypothesis has been confirmed. If your results are unexpected, then you've made a discovery. Both outcomes are equally important.

We learn just as much when we're proven wrong as we do when we're proven right. In some cases, we learn *more*.

You shouldn't use the Hypothesis Progression Framework as a scorecard to determine which team member "has the right answers." If you're doing this, you're missing the point.

The HPF should be used for continual learning and exploration. You should absolutely document when a hypothesis has been proven wrong. This will save everyone from treading on old ground or repeating the same mistakes. Create a culture that celebrates not just when a hypothesis has been validated, but also when a discovery has been made because a hypothesis has been invalidated.

A GREAT HYPOTHESIS REDUCES RISK

Note that when a hypothesis has been validated or invalidated, it doesn't become fact. You should think of hypotheses as an instrument to reduce risk. If you talk with 20 customers who all validate that your hypothesis is true, then you should feel as though you have greater confidence that it is. Therefore, you must continually test your hypotheses to "de-risk" your product strategy. By validating or invalidating what you know to be true, you grow your understanding of what *may* be successful and what *may not* be.

A validated hypothesis is not a guarantee, it's a window into what could *possibly* be true. You should prioritize accordingly. The riskier the decision you're trying to make, the more you want to try to validate the hypothesis that supports that decision.

We should strive to have the highest possible confidence in what we know to be true *before* we launch. It allows us to set expectations, position our products effectively, and better predict the outcome.

A GREAT HYPOTHESIS IS SPECIFIC

When working with teams, writing hypotheses for the first time, we find they try to "cast a wide net." The belief is that if their hypotheses are applicable to more people, it stands a greater chance of being validated or invalidated. Having a nonspecific hypothesis leads to nonspecific answers.

Let's go back to our previous example: working on a website that helps customers find local services providers like lawncare, childcare, and petsitting.

Let's say we want explore why customers might use this type of website. So we decide to try to validate the following hypothesis:

> People want to save money on services.

There's a high likelihood that this hypothesis will be validated. After all, who doesn't want to save money on services?! If we chose to use the validation of this hypothesis as justification to pursue our idea, we would be on shaky ground. In a sense, all we've validated is that people want to save money on services, not that they want to use a website to search for service providers.

Additionally, this type of general hypothesis will lead to uninformative conversations with our customers. It doesn't drill down to the specifics of the customer's motivation and will generate customer feedback that is all over the map or unhelpful.

Let's take another look at the Customer hypothesis template and see how it can be used to drive at a more specific hypothesis:

> We believe [type of customers] are motivated to [motivation] when doing [job-to-be-done].

> We believe working parents who have children under 12 are motivated to find quality childcare for an affordable price when searching the internet for service providers in their area.

What if we found this hypothesis to be *partially invalidated*? Imagine we talked to working mothers and we discovered that they didn't trust online searches when it came to their childcare needs; instead, they often preferred to use recommendations from their family and friends. They wanted to keep their search limited to people whose opinion they valued and trusted.

However, when we talked to fathers, we found that they valued having the greatest selection of results over personal recommendations. Fathers were more concerned about "missing out" on a great childcare provider, because none of their friends or family knew about it.

That would be an important discovery. We would want to iterate our hypothesis and start tracking mothers and fathers separately:

Invalidated

> We believe *working mothers* who have children under 12 are motivated to find quality childcare for an affordable price when searching the internet for service providers in their area.

Validated
> We believe *working fathers* who have children under 12 are motivated to find quality childcare for an affordable price when searching the internet for service providers in their area.

This segmentation will help us continually appreciate that mothers and fathers will use our site differently when it comes to searching for childcare services. It could affect the entire strategy of our website, what features we create, and how we target (or don't target) them to each customer segment.

That is why specific hypotheses are important. These subtle distinctions have huge consequences.

A GREAT HYPOTHESIS SEPARATES THE PERSON FROM THEIR BEHAVIOR

It's very easy to create an identity around someone's actions or behaviors. This can lead to convoluted hypotheses that are difficult to draw specific conclusions from. It can obfuscate underlying issues and motivations that are more critical.

For example, imagine we want to create a retention program to encourage customers not to leave our website that connects them to local service providers. We call these customers "churners"; they've created an account and engaged with the site for a couple of weeks, but haven't returned in over a month. We might have a hypothesis about why they haven't returned:

> We believe churners left our website because they are no longer looking for a service provider.

This seems like a legitimate reason for leaving our website; however, it's lacking because it focuses only on the behavior of churning—not *who the customers are* and *what motivated them to engage with us in the first place.*

How old are these churners? What is their level of skill or expertise with using the internet? Where do they live or work? What was their motivation for coming to our website in the first place? Did they fail to find a provider because there wasn't a desirable one in their area, or because the search tool was too confusing to navigate?

It's important to resist the urge to put the behaviors you're trying to correct (e.g., slow adoption, bad reviews, refusal to upgrade to paid service) in your hypotheses. It wraps the customer's identity around the negative behavior and makes it difficult to understand who they are and what truly motivates them.

If our strategy were to focus only on correcting behaviors that don't align with our business goals, we would end up distancing ourselves from our customers and fall into a combative "us verus them" mentality.

The key is to align our business goals with *their* goals.

A better hypothesis would be:

> We believe customers who have limited knowledge of the internet find it difficult to search for providers on our website, because they don't know what keywords can be used to narrow to produce meaningful results.

This hypothesis gets at the heart of the type of customer and the unique problem they're having (which is resulting in churn).

If this hypothesis were validated, we could explore how we might provide keyword suggestions to help customers conduct better searches or automatically provide customers with local providers without requiring them to conduct a search at all.

A GREAT HYPOTHESIS CAN BE MEASURED

Hypotheses must be measured objectively to determine their accuracy. Without these criteria, how do we know if our hypothesis has been validated or invalidated?

Imagine our goal is to help customers learn about premium features on our website. This is functionality that is available through a paid subscription. Let's say we had a hypothesis like this:

> We believe that customers using a free account are frustrated when searching for local service providers, because they need to see review comments, which are only provided through a paid subscription.

This is a good Problem hypothesis; however, what customer comments or behaviors will help us validate or invalidate whether it's true?

To help you measure and track your hypotheses, our playbooks rely on a blend of qualitative, quantitative, and "soft" quantitative data. Let's explore their unique differences.

Qualitative data

Effectively, this data is used to approximate or characterize your customers. It may be characteristic attributes or customer quotes that perfectly capture a common sentiment. We often say that while a picture is worth a thousand words, a direct customer quote can be worth ten thousand words.

Qualitative data helps you tell a rich and complete story that can raise your team's customer empathy. It brings customer depth by highlighting characteristics that allow you to make an emotional connection.

Imagine you're sharing with your leadership team something you learned from your customer development, regarding your paid subscription model.

You could say:

> We learned that our customers don't find the paid subscription valuable.

Or, you could share this direct quote from one of your customers:

> I really don't see the value of a paid subscription. I mean, you guys are charging a lot and most of the stuff I see here—these premium listing things—I mean, you should just be offering that for free. Look at your competitors! They offer all this stuff for free! Not only would I not pay for this, I would probably tell everyone to avoid your website, because you're clearly trying to rip people off. Seeing this kind of makes me angry, to be honest.

Which quote do you believe would compel your leadership team to act?

As you begin to talk with customers, it's important that you're not simply checking boxes and adding up totals, but that you're engaging in active listening and trying to capture their voice and unique perspectives.

These comments and quotes help enrich your data and boost your confidence that your hypothesis has been validated.

Quantitative data

During product development, we tend to rely on more traditional quantitative measures like satisfaction ratings or scores that determine intent to use. These numerical scores can be easily monitored and measured throughout your exploration.

You can certainly supplement the measurements we use in our playbooks with your own KPIs (key performance indicators), goals, or business metrics.

For example, you may have a survey asking customers to rate how valuable each of your premium subscription offerings is.

"Soft" quantitative data

"Soft" quantitative data is data that doesn't have statistical significance. These are numbers that allow us to track if there's a signal, without bringing in heavy formulas or statistical rigor. "Soft quant" measures are great when you're trying to measure the effectiveness of a design iteration or the number of times a sentiment is expressed by a customer.

For example, we may decide we're going to count the number of times customers express that a feature should be provided for free. If we talked to 10 service portal customers and 8 of them mentioned that our premium listings should be free, that would be a signal worth investigating.

Identifying measurable criteria for your hypotheses doesn't have to be complicated. Before testing your hypotheses, you should consider the signals you think you may hear from customers to either validate or invalidate your assumptions. One of the best ways to identify these types of signals is to formulate a Discussion Guide.

Formulating a Discussion Guide

The Discussion Guide is a tool that we use, in each of our playbooks, to help formulate the types of questions we will ask customers to validate our hypotheses. What questions we ask and, more importantly, how we ask them, is a critical component of how we test our hypotheses.

Having a solid strategy, before talking with customers, is a great way to ensure you and your team come back with meaningful results. We use our Discussion Guides to help teams have a shared understanding of the questions they want to have answered. Building the guide first ensures that teams are asking the same questions, in the same way, so that their results can be compared efficiently and effectively.

Let's go back to our example website that helps customers find service providers. Imagine we wanted to talk to customers about any negative experiences they may have had using our search engine.

If we were to ask, "What do you dislike about our search engine?" this, of course, implies that the customer disliked something. They may feel compelled to find something they didn't like, even if they thought the overall experience was fine. Effectively, we're biasing customers toward our conclusion that we believe something is wrong with our search engine experience. This type of question would only seek to confirm that bias, because customers may feel obligated to name something so they could properly answer our question. Here are some examples of nonleading questions that we could include in our Discussion Guide:

1. Tell me about the last time you tried to search for a provider on our website. What was that experience like?

2. How often are you able to successfully find a service provider you are looking for? How do you know you've been successful?

3. How confident do you feel when searching our site? Do you feel like you're able to find the best results? What makes you feel that way?

4. Have you ever had trouble finding a provider on our website? How did that make you feel?

5. If you could improve one thing about our search experience, what would it be?

Notice how these questions are open-ended. They don't evoke simple yes or no answers. Our Discussion Guides are intended to evoke a conversation. You want to open the space that you're exploring with customers and have them fill in the gaps with their own experiences and perspectives. Trust that customers will naturally talk about what matters to them, and structure your questions to help them do that.

Formulating Ideas

While we've emphasized the notion of formulating your assumptions into testable hypotheses and Discussion Guides, we also need a method to formulate product ideas.

As we navigate from customer development to product development, we need ways to help us generate ideas on how to effectively respond to the customer's problem. We employ activities like "How might we?" exercises, sketching, and storyboarding to help formulate ideas at this stage.

Key Points

- The best way to remain objective about your assumptions is to write hypotheses that can be tested with customer feedback.

- Each stage of the Hypothesis Progression Framework includes a hypothesis template that helps you formulate your assumptions into hypotheses. Each template is composed of parameters; some are shared throughout the framework, while others are unique to a specific stage.

- The [job-to-be-done] parameter, shared throughout the framework, is inspired by Clayton Christensen's Job Theory. His theory suggests that customers "hire" products to complete a job.

- A hypothesis that has been invalidated is just as valuable as one that has been validated. Invalidated hypotheses can prevent you from making costly mistakes or heading in a misguided direction.

- Writing hypotheses and validating them with customer data is all about reducing risk in your product decision-making. You'll never be 100% confident that a product decision will be a success, but by validating or invalidating your assumptions, you can increase your confidence that you're heading in the right direction.

- Hypotheses should be specific. Having a hypothesis that is too broad does not provide actionable information or insight. Including characteristics like the type of customer and their motivations, tasks, and frustrations will give you specific details that can help you make informed decisions.

- It's important to separate the person from the behavior you're trying to observe.

- Your hypotheses should have measurable criteria so that they can be effectively tested.

- A great hypothesis focuses on the *customer's* limitations, not your own. It's important that you don't inject your technical or political limitations into the customer's experience. For example, don't say, "Customers are frustrated because our search algorithm doesn't support location." Instead say, "Customers are frustrated when they cannot find specific search results using their location."

Endnotes

1 [gothelf] p. 23
2 [christensen] Chapter 2: Progress, Not Products

[3]

Experimenting

In the previous chapter, we discussed how we must identify our assumptions and formulate them into hypotheses that can be validated. Once we have our hypotheses, we'll be looking for ways that we can test them with customers.

A key component to our customer-driven strategy is maintaining an ongoing conversation with your customers. Interviews are a relatively cheap way to collect rich customer data, because you're hearing it "right from the source."

Interviewing best practices can be used whether you're conducting an interview, customer visit, focus group, concept value test, or usability test. Accordingly, the bulk of this chapter focuses on exploring interviews as an experimental method.

We'll also look at additional methods for collecting data and discuss their advantages and disadvantages.

Finally, we'll discuss how to find customers and how to have meaningful conversations with them.

Conducting a Successful Customer Interview

One of the key characteristics to any successful interview is preparation. While it may be tempting to jump in and start asking your customers questions, you'll be better served with a more structured approach. In Chapter 2, we talked about how you should take your hypotheses and formulate a Discussion Guide. We provide an example Discussion Guide in each of our playbooks, but let's look at some other techniques that can help you conduct great customer interviews.

Create a Screener

Before talking with customers, it's a good idea to have the team decide on the type of customer you want to talk to. While it might be tempting to say, "We're interested in talking with *anyone*," that doesn't set the foundation for a constructive interview. Having too broad of a segment doesn't allow you to focus your interview into a concise series of questions.

A screener is a series of specific questions that you can ask a customer *before* the interview to determine if they are the right fit for your study.

Let's revisit our example website that connects customers to service providers in their area. Say we're interested in finding out how well the relationships have been going between our customers and the local service providers they've contacted. We could set up a series of screener questions to ensure that we're talking to the best possible candidates for our study:

1. In the past six months, how often would you say you used our web portal?

2. In the past six months, how often would you say you searched for a service provider?

3. In the past six months, have you contacted a service provider to inquire about services?

4. In the past six months, have you scheduled an appointment with a service provider for consultation?

5. Are you currently receiving services from a provider you've contacted through our website?

If a customer answers "very often" or "yes" to these questions, there's a higher likelihood that they have enough experience with our portal to give us valuable insight into the relationships being established between our customers and service providers.

As a team, creating a screener can be a valuable exercise in determining what qualities you're looking for. Additionally, you can create multiple screeners and split different segments between team members. This will allow you to cover more ground and organize your team regarding who is talking with whom.

Give Time for Responses

When talking with customers, you may feel the urge to fill any silent moments with conversation. As an interviewer, you should be comfortable with "awkward silence" because it gives your customers a chance to reflect on the questions you're asking them.

If a customer says something interesting that you want to drill into, make a note of it and wait until they've completed their thought before asking a follow-up question.

You want to hear their stream-of-consciousness, unformatted responses. It's important to remain patient and not rush them to give you an answer or move the conversation along.

Remain Positive

During the interview, you want to exude positivity. Continually encourage feedback and reassure customers that they won't hurt your feelings with negative comments. The customer may feel like they're failing the interview because they're not telling you what you want to hear. You want to continually reassure them that any feedback is important and helpful, even when it's tough criticism.

Identify Roles During the Interview

While an interview can be conducted by a single person, we highly recommend having multiple team members join in. Not only is it good to have multiple people listening to the customer's responses, you can also use their help to facilitate the interview. However, be mindful that the customer might feel overwhelmed by the number of people on the call or in the room. You want your interview to feel like a personal conversation, not a congressional hearing.

If you have multiple people joining the customer interview, it's a good idea to assign roles so that everyone is aware of their responsibilities. Next we list some common roles that can be helpful during an interview.

MODERATOR

You should identify one person to moderate the interview. This eliminates the customer having to track multiple people during the call. If your team has questions they would like the moderator to ask during a call, have them send their question to the moderator via an instant message or, if you're in the same room, write the question on a dry-erase board or hand it over on a Post-it note (you can never have enough Post-it notes). If there's time available at the close of the interview, you can also open it up for any other member on your team to ask follow-up questions.

TIMEKEEPER AND COORDINATOR

A member from the team should be nominated to be timekeeper. If possible, have that person sit next to the moderator so they can quickly and quietly keep the moderator on schedule. Also, if you're planning on having the customer interview remotely, using an online conferencing tool like Microsoft Skype, Google Hangouts, or your own conferencing system, you should nominate this person to oversee the technology.

Timekeeping and logistics are a small thing, but you really want to help the moderator be engaged with the customer as much as possible. Keeping track of the time or fidgeting with technology can create distractions and break the flow of the conversation.

NOTE TAKER

The moderator should be free to focus on the interview script and keeping the conversation going. While you should encourage everyone other than the moderator to take notes, assign at least one person to the role of note taker. The note taker's responsibility is to capture everything they see and hear. Interpretation will come later, but for now, you want to capture everything that transpired during your visit with the customer.

Debrief

Plan to set aside 20–30 minutes after the interview for a team debrief. This is a critical time because the interview is still fresh in everyone's mind. You should give each person a chance to share what they've learned, while a note taker captures everyone's responses.

Here are some questions to think about while you're debriefing:

- What stood out to you the most; what was most surprising?

- What do you think motivates the customer? What are they trying to achieve?

- What is preventing the customer from achieving their goals?

- Did the customer express any problems or frustrations? What were they?

- What similarities or differences does this customer share with other customers?

How Many Customers Do I Need to Validate a Hypothesis?

When you're conducting interviews and looking for data to support your hypotheses, you may begin to ask yourself, "When do I know I have *enough* data?" As with any difficult question, there's a difficult answer: it depends. As we've discussed, the HPF and our Customer-Driven Cadence is an exercise in reducing risk. Therefore, you must determine, per project, how much risk you're willing to take.

For a minor feature upgrade, you may decide that talking with a handful of customers to make sure you've got it right is reasonable enough. If you're deciding on pivoting the product entirely, it may warrant a large pool of customers to ensure you've heard as many perspectives as possible.

Therefore, segmenting your customer base after you've talked with them is important. The parameters in the HPF will help you do that. You can segment your population based on their customer type, motivation, or problem, but you can also segment on organization, skillset, or a combination of these things. Segmenting your customers will ensure you've tracked exactly where the data points are coming from and help you identify if a group is over- or underrepresented.

Cindy Alvarez suggests you've done enough interviews if you start hearing the same thing over and over:[1]

> The best indicator that you're done is that you stop hearing people say things that surprise you. You'll feel confident that you've gotten good enough insights on your customers' common problems, motivations, frustrations, and stakeholders.

At first, you may find that your team disagrees on what you're hearing from customers. This is normal and expected. The key is to create an environment of mutual respect and shared understanding.

A great customer and product development strategy should employ *multiple* methods for collecting data. While we recommend that customer interviews should always be present in your strategy, we also encourage you to mix your methods for collecting data. For example, supplementing your interviews with a survey questionnaire is a great way to combine quantitative and qualitative feedback and complete your understanding of the customer.

We've explored how to use interviews as an experimental method for validating your hypotheses, but let's look at other methods you could use to collect customer data.

Surveys

Advantages

LARGE SAMPLE SIZE
Surveys can reach a greater number of respondents because they can be completed and distributed rather easily.

EASY ADMINISTRATION
Surveys are an unmoderated form of collecting customer responses to questions. In other words, you can give the survey to the respondents to complete themselves. This creates little overhead for you to administer the study and ensures consistency in how the questions are delivered.

There are many reasons to use surveys, but we've found they can be highly effective when used to:

Create a sample pool of customers
> If you have access to customers and you want to determine if they fit the customer type you're interested in, a survey is a great way to start the initial point of contact.

Generalize a hypothesis
> If you've found that a hypothesis appears to be validated during interviews, you can conduct a survey with a broader set of customers to see if your finding generalizes to a greater set of your customer base.

You can always use a survey as a guardrail for a customer interview. The nice thing about being able to talk to customers while they complete your survey is that they give you the "why" for their response.

EASY ANALYSIS

Survey tools create many useful ways to analyze and report on your data. Because most surveys today can be completed electronically, it's not uncommon to conduct real-time analysis as customers complete your survey.

Disadvantages

DIFFICULTY OF WRITING QUESTIONS

It can be hard to craft a survey question that will elicit the response you're looking for *and* be easy for the respondent to interpret correctly. Survey data can be heavily impacted by the types of questions you ask and how you ask them. With surveys, you rely heavily on the respondent's ability to understand the "spirit" of your question.

When we first start working with teams, we find that they typically want their initial conversation with a customer to be a survey. If they don't know a lot about the customer, they want to gather as much information as possible before engaging in a phone conversation. Intuitively, that seems like the right approach. Yet the minute the team starts to write their survey questions, they quickly realize they don't know what questions to ask and how to ask them.

The better approach is to start talking to customers as soon as possible. You still may not know the perfect questions to ask, but it gives you an opportunity to quickly revise your question until the customer understands what you're trying to learn.

MORE QUESTIONS THAN ANSWERS

Surveys can give you a "quick read" of a bulk of responses. They can easily tell you *what* respondents said, but not *why* they said it. We often find that when teams use surveys, they inevitably end up with many more follow-up questions. That's why surveys should be used as a tool to "test the waters" or give you a general feeling of a group. Following up a survey with a series of interviews will help you understand the meaning behind their responses. Therefore, it's good idea to conclude the survey with a question that asks, "Would you be willing for us to contact you regarding your responses to this survey?" and ask respondents to leave contact information.

Analytics

Analytics could be anything from counting the number of times a customer clicks on a button in your app or the number of customers calling your customer support line.

Advantages

LARGE SAMPLE SIZE OF ACTUAL CUSTOMERS

Analytics gives you the widest possible access to your customer base. By tracking customers' behaviors, you'll be able to gain insight into how they are using your products. Additionally, there is little to no barrier or friction for the customer.

A/B TESTING

Using analytics you can set up experiments within your product. You can try different configurations and experiences, and measure if they result in the behavior you're looking for. This can be a low-cost way to test the validity of your ideas on real customers using your product.

Disadvantages

DIFFICULTY OF CORRELATING USAGE WITH CUSTOMER INTENT

While analytics can give you an indication of *what* is happening, it'll never answer *why* it's happening. Inferring a customer's motivation from their usage can leave major gaps in your understanding.

For example, let's return to our website that helps customers find service providers in their area. We've added a new "Free 30-day subscription" banner, near the login button. Analytics is suggesting that a small number of customers are selecting the banner. We might assume that the location or visibility of the new banner is poor, resulting in fewer clicks. It may seem like a good idea to increase visibility by making the banner more prominent on the page.

However, after talking with customers, we find the actual reason they are not clicking on the banner is because their primary motivation when they come to our site is to find service providers in their area—not to think about subscribing to the premium features. They tell us they want to try the product first and have us reveal premium features, progressively, as they use the product.

Analytics is a low-cost way to look for signals that can help guide your formulation of assumptions and hypotheses, but interviews and focus groups almost always help explain the data and find deeper meaning. That's why analytics should be used to cross-triangulate results from other customer and product development research.

Focus Groups

Advantages

INTERESTING CUSTOMER INTERACTION
It can be great to have participants interact and share with each other. In some cases, one customer's comment generates a new idea or thought from another customer; or hearing one person's frustration might embolden someone to share a similar experience where they might not have otherwise. This type of interaction can lead to a livelier and more engaging feedback session.

Focus groups can help if you're interested in learning group dynamics, like how a professional team collaborates on a project or how classmates help each other with homework.

MORE INTERVIEWS IN THE SAME AMOUNT OF TIME
If you're short on time and cannot commit to running a single interview with each person individually, getting multiple people on the same call can help save time.

Disadvantages

DIFFICULTY OF MANAGING A GROUP
It can be difficult to manage a group of people while asking for their feedback. A single comment can take the group "off the rails" as they spend all their time distracted by something that isn't irrelevant to your study. A skilled moderator can gently guide the group to ensure that the conversation stays on course.

INFLUENCE OF GROUPTHINK

Having a group of customers provide feedback can generate an engaging conversation and the sharing of alternative ideas. However, you should also be mindful of the effects of *groupthink*, a mode of thinking in a cohesive group where members strive for agreement rather than appreciating alternative courses of action.[2]

During focus groups, customers may respond as a cohesive group rather than expressing their individual opinions. You may find that they are reluctant to say or do anything that may disrupt the group, such as voicing criticisms against the ideas or opinions of other group members.[3]

A skilled moderator will see signals that groupthink is occurring. These might include:

Strong personalities

A single person with a strong or vocal personality can begin to persuade the group as a whole.

Cohesion

The group might "band together" to avoid conflict and appear they are unified in their thinking.

Diverse skillsets or abilities

Each person has their own set of experiences and skills they bring to the focus group. Inexperienced customers may shy from voicing their opinion, for fear of sounding inferior or uninformed.

Moderators limit these issues by ensuring that everyone has a chance to speak, continually checking for agreement (e.g., by asking "Does anyone have a different opinion?"), and modifying questions so that everyone, regardless of experience level, can contribute to the conversation.

CHALLENGING LOGISTICS

Depending on the audience you're targeting, it can be challenging to schedule participants all at the same time. Conducting focus groups remotely, using an online videoconference solution, can help reduce the time required to get a group of people together.

Customer Visits

Advantages

UNIQUE PERSPECTIVES

It's one thing to hear a customer describe their environment, but another thing entirely to see it for yourself. Customer visits are the highest-fidelity and deepest customer learning you can experience. With customer visits, you can immerse yourself in the customer's world and truly get a sense of the problems they face. It's a great way to create a boost in customer empathy, as the team no longer needs to imagine what the customer is experiencing; they can see it for themselves.

OBSERVATION OF EXTERNAL FACTORS

We often become so focused on fixing the problems our customers tell us about that we forget there are external factors that customers may be completely unaware of. Being able to observe your product "in the wild" can offer new insights that you hadn't previously considered. For example, a customer who uses your smartwatch in a noisy office setting might not think to mention that it's hard to hear audio from the speaker, because they think it's an issue that is unique to them, not to the product. When you go into their office, you notice that they frequently leave their desk to go to a quiet room to interact with the watch. You might wonder why the customer never thought to mention that, but to the customer, it has become part of their routine, so it's just an insignificant detail. These types of discoveries can be game changers in your product's strategy.

Disadvantages

COST

Depending on where your customer base is located, it can be costly to make travel arrangements. To save on cost, you might consider sending a smaller team with a set of cameras (assuming it's okay with your customer to record video of their environment). We've had success using wide-angle cameras from companies like GoPro. They're small and unobtrusive, and the wide-angle lens provides the ability to capture more of the physical space in the recording.

DIFFICULTY OF GAINING ACCESS

Depending on the sensitivity of your customer's work, you may find it difficult to get the proper clearance for you and your team to be onsite. Additionally, gaining access to the customer's time may be difficult. Ideally, you'll want to see them at their peak, when they're using your product to its fullest potential. However, these peaks might be precisely the time your customer doesn't want any distractions. They may prefer instead that your team visit when they have downtime, which runs counter to your reasons for visiting.

Usability Tests

Advantages

PRECISION

Depending on how you design it, you can control the variables in your study. With usability tests, you can set up the "perfect conditions" for your customer to operate in. This helps you isolate variables and focus on the things you care about.

DIRECTNESS

Watching the customer try to accomplish tasks using your product is one of the most direct ways to test its success. If possible, include the people that are developing the product. Having them watch customers struggle, become frustrated, or give up is a powerful motivator to fix a problem. Usability tests are a great fast track to customer empathy, because the team gets to see the direct consequence of their design decisions.

Disadvantages

NARROWNESS

Usability tests can tend to fixate on a product's ability to "succeed" in getting a customer from A to B. However, just because a product is usable doesn't mean it's *useful*. Some people think that just because a feature passes usability tests, it will be something customers want. We've seen countless examples where a product is easy to use, but simply doesn't create value for customers. Bottom line: usability tests help answer the question *"Can they use it?"* but not *"Will they use it?"*

Depending on the nature of your product or the customer you serve, it can be costly to get in front of customers and watch them try your products or prototypes. You can certainly conduct usability tests remotely (we do it all the time), but that really depends on the nature of what you're trying to accomplish.

Many teams make the mistake of starting their customer development at the usability testing stage. At this point, they've already built something and are overly invested in the study's success. Customer feedback is almost moot because the team is already committed to shipping what they've built.

That's why experimenting at all stages of the Hypothesis Progression Framework is so critically important. Engaging with customers early, before you've built anything, is the best way to avoid costly mistakes.

How to Find Customers

We've found that social networks like LinkedIn, Twitter, Reddit, and Facebook are great networks to leverage when trying to find customers. You can also leverage local user groups, meetups, or conferences to help build your list of customer contacts.

Leveraging your product's existing support channels can be helpful as well. If you have support forums or a support hotline, you may consider using these resources to identify customers with a certain motivation or problem. We also find that offering direct support can be a great, inexpensive way to get a customer to talk with you.

For example, if a customer is having an issue with logging in, you could put them in contact with a support technician to help them. Once the issue is resolved, you could ask if the customer would be willing to share a few more moments of their time to go over some questions. Customers tend to be more agreeable if you've just helped them with an issue they were having, so this is a great way to turn a customer support call into a customer interview.

Getting the Customer's Attention

Probably one of the most difficult tasks you'll have, when reaching out to a customer, is overcoming their suspicion that you're trying to sell them something. We've all been inundated with countless telemarketers, sales promotions, or giveaways to the point that we've created a "noise filter," automatically disregarding any communication that sounds like a sales pitch.

Unfortunately, when you try to contact a customer, especially over email, you'll have to overcome those filters to get a customer's attention. Here are some tips that can help.

Update Your Online Profile

Depending on how tech savvy your customer is, they might look you up on various social networks. Therefore, it's a good idea to ensure that your social networking accounts are up-to-date. For instance, if you reach out to a customer as a representative of your company, make sure your LinkedIn and Twitter profiles have been updated to show that you do, in fact, work for the company.

We've also found that an updated profile picture makes a big difference. It may sound funny, but having a nice profile picture, with your smiling face, can go a long way toward a customer believing that you're a real person who's interested in their feedback.

Favor Depth over Breadth

You might be tempted to do an email blast, or mass communication, as it can seem like the sure-fire way to "catch" the most number of customers in a single message. The problem with this approach is that these communications tend to find their way into customers' spam filters, or get completely ignored. It's tough to be personal and authentic when your email sounds like it has been formatted with the broadest possible audience in mind.

We like to do a bit of work investigating a potential customer prior to making the first contact. It can take more time up front, but it tends to produce a higher-quality group of participants in the long run.

Let's return to our example website that connects customers to service providers in their area. Imagine we're working on a feature that helps teach customers about the types of things they should look for when considering a provider for services like lawn care, house cleaning, or home repair.

We search Twitter and come across a tweet that references a blog post discussing the frustration of finding a qualified professional for home care services. The post has been retweeted over 1,000 times and has been liked nearly 5,000 times. This would certainly be a positive signal that this problem is something that resonates with many potential customers.

We could reach out to the author to tell her we appreciate the article and ask if she'd be willing to let us contact her. We could explain that we're investigating ways we can help our customers find qualified service providers and, because of her blog post, we think she could give us a lot of insight. If she's written a blog post about it, there's a high likelihood that she's passionate about finding a resolution to the problem. There's a good chance that she'd be motivated to partner with us in finding a solution. This type of communication is meaningful and personal. It sounds less like a sales pitch and shows that we have a genuine interest solving the customer's frustration. We're establishing a *relationship* with her, based on our common goals. Additionally, if she has a strong following on Twitter, she would make a great partner in helping us spread the word if we eventually do offer the new feature.

We could also look at the thousands of people that retweeted, liked, or commented on her article. These could also be potential leads for us to follow up on.

Therefore, a single tweet or blog post could foster many high-value customers for upcoming interviews. When you're recruiting, it's best to go into the process with the mindset that you're trying to find customers that you can partner with. If possible, you want to establish long-term relationships that will continually provide value through your ongoing feedback loop.

Reward Participation with "Exclusivity"

If you work on a product team, you should absolutely mention that in your communication. We find that customers like the idea that they've been contacted directly by the people who make the products they use. Be sure to tell them why they've been selected and be specific about how you believe they can help you and other customers.

Cindy Alvarez suggests that human beings are all motivated by three simple desires:[4]

- We like to help others.

- We like to sound smart.

- We like to fix things.

We find this to be true as well. Any time we position the customer as the expert, we find they have a greater sense of duty and engagement. They feel empowered and have a greater desire to get involved and offer their expertise.

We've even created "insider programs" or "customer councils" and invited some of our more vocal customers to participate. Customers like the distinction of being involved in an exclusive group or feeling like they have a say in the direction of the product you're building. As a reward, we elevate their status, offering a direct line with our product team or an opportunity to see new features before they're released.

These types of programs serve as a complete win-win for the product group and our enthusiastic customers.

Key Points

- Direct customer interviews are a low-cost way to collect rich customer feedback.

- Knowing when you've collected enough information to validate or invalidate your hypothesis is completely dependent on the goals for your project. A good rule of thumb is to weigh the cost of your product or feature idea against the cost of collecting the customer data. You typically know you've talked to enough customers when you hear the same responses from customers and gain no new information or insights. If that's the case, consider moving on or asking different questions.

- It's a good idea to create a screener, a set of questions that determine whether a customer is the right participant for your study.

- In-person interviews allow you to observe body language and see how engaged customers are. Remote interviews using online videoconferencing software can save you time and travel costs.

- When interviewing customers, give them time to think and respond to your question. Be comfortable with "awkward silences" and let interviewees complete a response before following up with another question.

- A great interview should be a positive experience for your customer. Continually encourage and thank them for their feedback, even when their comments are negative and critical.

- Have more than one person available during an interview. However, you should assign roles: a single moderator, a note taker, and a timekeeper.

- Leave a bit of time after the interview to debrief with your team. This will allow the team to share what they learned while it's still fresh in their mind.

- Surveys can give you many responses and are easy to distribute, but depending on the questions you ask, the results can leave you with more questions than answers.

- Analytics does a good job of telling you *what* customers are doing with your products, but it does a poor job of telling you *why* they are doing it.

- Focus groups provide a way for customers to interact and share perspectives with one another. However, they require a skilled moderator to ensure one or two voices don't dominate the discussion.

- Customer visits can give you a unique opportunity to observe your customers in their environment, but they can be costly and difficult to coordinate.

- Having a great customer and product development strategy requires having customers that you can talk to. Customers might be hesitant to talk to you because they think you'll try to sell them something. Therefore, you should ensure that your communication is specific and personal, not generic and automated.

- You can find customers on popular social networking sites like Twitter, LinkedIn, and Facebook. You can also create "insider groups" where you reward customers for their feedback with access to support or a chance to see new features.

Endnotes

1   [alvarez] p. 125
2   [janis] p. 9
3   [janis-political-psychology]
4   [alvarez] pp. 32–33

[4]

Sensemaking

In March 2011, David Moore published a sensemaking manual to help central intelligence agencies reduce *mindlessness*, a mode of fixation and relaxation where analysts became "so preoccupied with a few central signals that they largely ignored things in their periphery."[1]

Moore observed that analysts had developed an automatic response to the signals they were seeing, which prevented them from uncovering new insights. To keep up with the wealth of incoming data, they began to focus on specific signals, leaving themselves vulnerable to new threats they hadn't considered.

As you begin to conduct interviews, surveys, concept value tests, and other experiments, your team will have a flood of data points. It can be hard to gain broad insights from all of these signals and, just like intelligence analysts, your team will be susceptible to focusing on just a few signals, missing out on larger opportunities for your products.

Sensemaking is a process that ensures we organize the data we collect, identify patterns and meaningful insights, and refine them into a story that compels others to action.

The Sensemaking Loop

Sensemaking is a perpetual cycle of collecting data, making sense out of it, and sharing knowledge throughout our teams and organizations. Pirolli and Card refer to this as the "sensemaking loop."[2] It essentially breaks down into five procedural components (see Figure 4-1):

- Data sources
- Shoebox
- Evidence file
- Schema
- Stories

FIGURE 4-1

The sensemaking loop

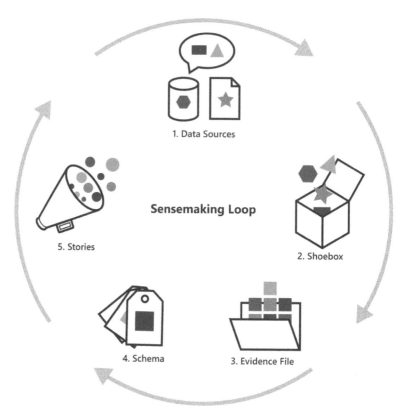

These components come together to help you transition raw customer data into meaningful, "sticky" insights. You'll find that, in our playbooks, we provide activities that help you navigate this loop by taking your data, curating an evidence file, creating schemas, and crafting a compelling story to share throughout your organization.

You can think of the sensemaking loop as the components you'll need to make an effective case for your product's strategy. The hypotheses you create with the HPF will be the backbone of this loop.

Sensemaking is a continuous cycle that we use at every stage of the HPF. Each stage will manifest its own insights. While it isn't close to an exhaustive list, Table 4-1 gives some examples.

TABLE 4-1. Types of insights you'll gain by doing sensemaking at each stage of the HPF

HPF STAGE	INSIGHTS
Customer	Population characteristics (age, experience, skills, etc.), context/environment, current behaviors, motivations
Problem	Patterns of need or opportunity, process breakdowns, common ways customers are solving a problem, feelings and emotions
Concept	Usefulness, most important benefits, "dealbreaking" limitations, likelihood of use, shared values
Feature	Interaction issues, broken workflows, changes in satisfaction

As you engage in sensemaking, you'll find that it's not a linear path, where you move from collecting data to sharing your knowledge. Instead, you'll move back and forth within the loop—collecting data, identifying patterns, sharing stories, and returning to collect more data.

Put another way, sensemaking isn't a destination, where you try to reach the end of the loop; it's a continual process that ensures consistent learning and a fully developed understanding of your customers.

Let's look at each component of the loop more closely.

Data Sources

We've talked about the various methods you can employ to validate your hypotheses. While most of the types of experiments we've discussed have talking to customers at their heart, your customer and product development strategy should pull from multiple data sources.

Usage statistics, discussion forums, support tickets, and customer relationship management (CRM) systems are all great sources for data. You can also forage through market trend analysis reports, conduct a competitive analysis, or go on a customer visit. The important thing here is that while you're making sense of the data you're collecting, you're also tracking the sources of that data.

Shoeboxes

Before the advent of cloud storage and digital photography, the shoebox was the de facto storage method for photos. Shoeboxes were great because they required little to no organization (you could just wrap a rubber band around the photos from your summer vacation), and they kept all your photos secure and in the same place.

As you begin to cull your data sources, you'll collect notes, articles, and other assets that comprise your area of study. There are many online collaborative "shoeboxes" to store these types of things. Microsoft SharePoint, OneNote, Evernote, Basecamp, Google Drive, and Dropbox are all tools that allow teams to collect the information they're gathering. You shouldn't spend too much time curating or organizing your shoebox. This should be a loose inventory of any data you've collected—important or unimportant.

Evidence Files

When you're on a customer or product development journey, you're running an investigation. Your evidence file is like a case file: it contains the meaningful bits of data that comprise your point of view, vision, or strategy for your product.

An evidence file could include pictures of a customer's environment, a direct customer quote, or any other type of signal that points to why you validated or invalidated your hypotheses. For example, you could begin to capture direct quotes from your customer interviews that highlight a particular motivation or problem you hypothesized might exist.

These evidence files should be constantly culled, organized, and reflected upon, as they are the foundation for the case you're trying to make on behalf of your customer. They can help the team stay organized and up-to-date on the latest findings.

As you begin to curate your evidence files, you'll find yourself adding pieces of evidence that your gut tells you are meaningful but you're not yet sure why. Your ability to clearly articulate the underlying meaning will evolve as the evidence file takes shape. You'll find yourself continually moving things back and forth between your shoebox and evidence file until you've refined your collection to its most impactful bits of data.

When starting your project, you may find that *all* the data you've collected feels meaningful, and that's okay. As your project matures, you'll need a way to reduce your data signals and separate the "wheat from the chaff." What you believe to be most meaningful will evolve over time, and so should your evidence file.

Schemas

Schematizing data is the process of applying categories and patterns to your data. We often refer to this as "tagging your data," giving it meaning and defining it.

For example, you may mark a quote with a "problem" tag when a customer expresses a frustration. This will help you look at all your interviews and identify each time a frustration was articulated.

These tags will help you see patterns in your data and begin to draw conclusions.

Again, the parameters within the HPF automatically get you started. If your hypotheses and Discussion Guides are formulated to capture parameters like job-to-be-done, problem, or motivation, it can be much easier to begin tagging your data using those parameters.

We've repeatedly seen teams create spreadsheets to connect the data they've collected to their hypotheses. Some spreadsheets are quite simple, tracking the status of hypotheses. Others are more elaborate, containing dashboard-like interfaces with counters and formatting that change the status of a hypothesis from green to red based on the number of times it has been validated or invalidated.

We've also seen teams create hypotheses backlogs that help them track the various hypotheses the team might be exploring (and remember others they stopped exploring).

Stories

There are two things you need to get others onboard with your vision:

- A compelling story

- A way to share it

The most important thing about sensemaking is that it helps you share *meaning*, not data. Data is important, but emotion and empathy are what compel others to action.

As you begin to identify patterns, you'll need ways to express your data so that people can easily understand it. Visual elements like charts, graphs, and models can be a powerful way to help others understand what you've learned.

You can certainly take the quantitative data you've collected and transfer it into pie charts or line graphs, but you should look for more illustrative models as well. For example, you may have identified that there is a tension between customers wanting quality service providers and saving money. Perhaps this tension changes, depending on the type of service the customer is looking for. A customer might be looking to save money when researching lawn care service, but willing to pay much more for quality childcare.

Illustrating these nuances in graphical models can help others easily understand relationships and connections in your data.

Analogies and metaphors are also powerful tools to help convey complex ideas to others. Look for opportunities where your findings parallel other situations that might be more familiar and accessible to them. For example, one of our teams identified parallels between people trying to learn a new programming language and people learning to swim. This comparison helped the rest of the organization empathize with how difficult the challenges were without requiring knowledge about the programming language.

Once you have a compelling story, you need a way to share it with others in your organization. You'll want to create a continuous communication channel (or multiple channels) that's easy to use and accessible to everyone. We've found the less formal and lightweight the communication channel is, the more likely people are to use it. Leverage existing channels like email or chat clients so you don't have to encourage your organization to use another channel they can easily ignore.

Throughout the stages in the HPF, you should fall into a pattern of continual sensemaking; these activities should be happening, in parallel, with your customer and product development. You can do this by splitting the teams' efforts or scheduling a day each week, during development, to stop and make sense of the data you've been collecting.

Over time, the continual pattern of the sensemaking loop will increase your understanding and the overall empathy of your organization toward its customers.

At this point, we've covered the three phases of the Customer-Driven Cadence: Formulating, Experimenting, and Sensemaking. This cadence happens in each stage of the HPF. You formulate your assumptions into hypotheses, you run experiments to collect data, and you make sense of that data to gain insights.

Now, we're going to dive into each stage of the HPF and examine the hypotheses and parameters we use to drive us toward better understanding our customers, their problems, and what they find valuable and useful.

Key Points

- Sensemaking is the process you go through to take your raw customer data and convert it into meaningful results that can be shared with others.

- The sensemaking loop is a series of components that make up the sensemaking processes. These components include external data sources, shoeboxes, evidence files, schemas, and stories.

- External data sources are an inventory of the sources of the data you're collecting. While our playbooks focus primarily on direct customer interactions, you may also have supporting data coming from market reports, competitive analysis, discussion forums, support tickets, or customer relationship management systems.

- The shoebox is the location where you store all your interview notes, articles, pictures, or any other assets that have been generated throughout your customer and product development.

- The evidence file is your curated and organized location for the findings that validate or invalidate your hypotheses. Much like investigators, you will need an evidence file to help your team make their case. Some teams use spreadsheet software, formulas, and special formatting to connect their data points to a validated or invalidated hypothesis.

- Storytelling is an essential component of the customer-driven processes. By using charts, graphs, models, and illustrations, you can share your findings with a broader audience. Metaphors and analogies can be used to draw parallels between a complex learning and something that is more accessible or understandable to your audience.

- To surface your learnings, you'll need to support multiple channels for sharing information. Some teams use daily or weekly standups, monthly newsletters, or email aliases where team members can share their customer interview notes.

Endnotes

1 [moore] p. xxiv
2 [pirolli]

[5]

The Customer

2012 was a tough year for T-Mobile. They suffered a major embarrassment when their merger with AT&T failed to get the necessary regulatory approval; and due to the company's uncertain future, lack of support for the iPhone, and poor network coverage, they lost 800,000 subscribers.[1] This was a death knell for the small US wireless company, which had been trying to compete with the likes of behemoths like Verizon and AT&T. Many believed that T-Mobile's days were numbered.

At the beginning of 2013, CEO John Legere took the stage and announced that the company was headed in a new direction. He proclaimed that T-Mobile was going to be the country's "un-carrier."[2]

Legree argued that consumers were frustrated with complex calling and texting plans, long-term contracts, and confusing surcharges. T-Mobile was committed to doing business differently, and their goal was to be unlike any other mobile carrier—by not acting like a carrier at all.

On stage, Legere was bombastic, and at times vulgar, when describing the frustrations customers encountered when dealing with T-Mobile's competitors. He wanted people to understand that he got their frustrations.

T-Mobile was going to be different. They were going to speak plainly and honestly, and above all else, they were going to do right by their customers.

Along with pumping four billion into upgrading their 4G LTE rollout, T-Mobile introduced their Simple ChoicePlan, which asked customers two simple questions: how many lines do you need, and how much data do you want? This plan was simple to understand and, more importantly, completely void of any contracts or legal jargon.

This was a radical departure from what the competition was doing (see Figure 5-1). Instead of hiding behind outrageous contracts and complex legalese where they could hide fees and conspicuously raise rates, T-Mobile was going to make their offerings clear and simple. No games, no tricks, just wildly great customer service.

FIGURE 5-1

Mike Sievert, COO of T-Mobile, showing the complexity of the competition's wireless plans

The "un-carrier" approach, with its bold colors and edgy advertising, had a strong impact on customers' perceptions of the company. T-Mobile had tapped into many customers' frustrations with their current providers, and appeared to be empathetic and sincere in trying to improve their situation.

T-Mobile could not compete head-to-head with its competitors when it came to device selection or network coverage, but customers were beginning to value T-Mobile as the authentic and scrappy underdog.

That year, T-Mobile grew their subscriber base for the first time in 4 years and, for the next 13 consecutive quarters, maintained over 1 million added subscribers each quarter.[3]

In short order, T-Mobile went from being at death's door to being the country's fastest-growing wireless company.[4] Additionally, the company enjoyed outstanding customer satisfaction ratings, continually topping the list when compared to the competition.

By focusing on the motivations and desires of their customers, T-Mobile completely turned their company around. Instead of being a small wireless carrier, pushed around in a dominated industry, they became a customer-driven contender. Eventually, Verizon and AT&T had to modify their offerings because many of their customers were leaving for T-Mobile's simple, contract-free pricing.

Formulating a Customer Hypothesis

Like T-Mobile, the most successful companies are continually trying to answer three fundamental questions about their customers:

- Who is the customer?
- What do they want to achieve?
- How can we help them?

During the Customer stage of the HPF, we're trying to answer the first two questions (the Concept stage helps us answer the third question). We do this by formulating hypotheses that reflect our assumptions and then test these beliefs with our customers.

Let's look at the hypothesis template that is applied at the Customer stage:

> We believe [type of customers] are motivated to [motivation] when doing [job-to-be-done].

As discussed in Chapter 2, each hypothesis template, at every stage, contains the parameters [type of customers] and [job-to-be-done]. The Customer stage is where you'll begin to define and segment the customer you believe you're targeting. Through validating and invalidating your Customer hypotheses, you'll have a better understanding of who your customer is, what they're trying to do, and why they're motivated to do it. Let's look at the three parameters of the Customer hypothesis template more closely.

Types of Customers

No two people are alike. So we shouldn't group all our customers into two simple buckets: those who are using our products and those who are not. If we do that, we will miss all the nuances in between.

When we formulate our Customer hypothesis, we want to be sure that the [type of customers] parameter isn't defined by the customer's problem, the task they're doing, or the product they're using. This parameter should reflect the customer's identity.

In their book *Lean Enterprise,* authors Jez Humble, Joanne Molesky, and Barry O'Reilly suggest the most effective way to segment customers is to "pinpoint a cause and effect relationship between a person's characteristics and his or her interest in in your offering."[5] In other words, you want to identify unique attributes of customers who are or are not interested in your products.

Cindy Alvarez says that you should not become overreliant on traditional labels, like marketing demographics.[6] Age, gender, ethnicity, and location are important, but these attributes do not completely define your customer.

Identifying motivations, interests, unique perspectives, and behaviors is much more powerful and insightful than a list of generic demographic information. Therefore, being specific about the type of customer will lead to greater clarity when you're making sense of the data you've collected and sharing what you've learned. Let's look at an example.

Imagine we're members of a team working on a desktop publishing tool. Our tool, called StarDoc, allows customers to create flyers, newsletters, calendars, and business documents like memos and letters. Our team is looking for new opportunities to help small businesses with document creation.

When creating Customer hypotheses, we want to make sure that we're separating the customer from the product.

For example, we shouldn't begin our Customer hypothesis by saying:

> We believe StarDoc users are motivated to [motivation] when doing [job-to-be-done].

We would say:

> We believe office administrators working for small businesses are motivated to [motivation] when doing [job-to-be-done].

Effectively, the customer has an identity beyond the fact that they use StarDoc. It's important to capture that identity so we know, specifically, whom we're talking about when we refer to this segment of our customer base.

Motivation

Throughout our day, we make thousands of tiny little decisions to achieve an outcome. Sometimes these decisions are made in a blink of an eye, and others are thoughtfully mulled over and considered.

The underlying stream that supports these decisions is our motivation. We use products and purchase services because we're motivated to achieve a certain outcome. T-Mobile understood that customers were motivated to avoid lengthy and complex contracts, and this understanding helped the company stand out from their competitors.

Let's go back to our example of office administrators working for small businesses. We think that these administrators have a strong desire to create promotional brochures for their businesses. We might be inclined to continue our Customer hypothesis by saying:

> We believe office administrators working for small businesses are motivated to make a promotional brochure when doing [job-to-be-done].

However, when you look at this hypothesis, it feels like it's missing a *higher-level* motivation. Sure, the customer's goal is to make a promotional brochure, but the first questions that come to mind are, "Why do they want to create a brochure? What are they hoping it will accomplish?"

After talking with office administrators about their desire to create brochures, we learn that many of them are struggling to find low-cost ways to promote their business offerings. So, we revise our Customer hypothesis to capture that motivation:

> We believe office administrators working for small businesses are motivated to promote their business offerings when doing [job-to-be-done].

By capturing the higher-level motivation, we've opened our hypothesis up to many more opportunities. This will help us explore various jobs our office administrators will "hire," using our product, to advance their goal of promoting their business.

Job-to-Be-Done

As discussed in Chapter 2, the [job-to-be-done] captures the tasks that customers will engage in to achieve their goals.

Let's consider our office administrators trying to create promotional brochures. Under the Jobs Theory, we would say the product that the office administrators "hired" to complete the job of creating a brochure was StarDoc.

At this point, you may be thinking, "This seems like a lot of word-play and semantics," and you'd be right. However, the words we use strongly affect our understanding of what we're trying to help customers achieve. Therefore, it's important for us to clarify, with language as specific as possible, what we are (and are not) doing to help a customer achieve their goal.

So, let's try to plug StarDoc into our job-to-be-done, within our Customer hypothesis:

> We believe office administrators working for small businesses are motivated to promote their business offerings when using StarDoc.

You may have noticed we've changed the verb from *doing* to *using*. From time to time, you'll find that you need to change the HPF templates to make them easier to read or understand. Again, these templates should serve only as an example. You're free to rework them however you'd like; it's the hypothesis *parameters* we strongly encourage you to keep.

The job-to-be-done in this hypothesis focuses on the product (StarDoc) rather than the task (creating a promotional brochure). Therefore, we want to articulate what job the customer is "hiring" to promote their business offering. In this case, we believe the customer has chosen a brochure to achieve their goal:

> We believe office administrators working for small businesses are motivated to promote their business offerings when creating promotional brochures.

This completed Customer hypothesis sheds light on the type of customer, their motivation, and the job they're engaged in. We could now run an experiment on this hypothesis by talking with office administrators about how they promote their businesses. We could then determine if they engage in activities like creating brochures.

We could have several variants of this hypothesis with different job-to-be-done parameters, such as creating posters, creating flyers, or creating newsletters. These variants could happen with any one of the Customer parameters.

For example, there could be many jobs or tasks employed by office administrators to help them promote their business (Figure 5-2).

Types of Customers	Motivations	Jobs-to-be-Done	
		Create an ad for a local newspaper	**FIGURE 5-2** Jobs that may be "hired" to promote business offerings
		Create a website	
Office administrator for a small business	Promote business offerings	Create a brochure	
		Create a monthly newsletter	
		Create a sign or banner	

The StarDoc team could identify many types of customers, motivations, and jobs. Some of the motivations and jobs may be unique to a specific customer type; others may be shared across multiple customer types (Figure 5-3).

This is why segmenting your customer base is so important: so you don't mix the signals you're hearing from one group and generalize them to other groups.

FIGURE 5-3
Various types of
customers, motivations,
and jobs

Types of Customers	Motivations	Jobs-to-be-Done
Student who has recently graduated	Looking for new job opportunities	Create a resume
Electrician running his own business	Organize billing to secure revenue	Create an invoice
Entrepreneur starting a new company	Looking to attract investors	Create business cards
Office administrator for a small business	**Promote business offerings**	**Create a brochure**
Director of a nonprofit organization	Keep donors involved and active	Create a monthly newsletter

Throughout the remaining chapters, we're going to revisit PartyTime Apps. They were the team we presented at the opening of this book that were given 10 weeks to find ways they could "triple revenue" for the company. We're going to see how they could use the HPF and the Customer-Driven Cadence to tackle this challenge.

PartyTime Apps Revisited

"Over the next 10 weeks, we want you to come up with product ideas that can attract new customers and *triple* our revenue."

After Susan and her team got over the shock of such an audacious request, the team agreed that they needed to get organized quickly.

As a team, they began to formulate their assumptions about the types of customers they could engage for new business opportunities. The team began listing every customer attribute they could think of.

In less than an hour, the team had covered a wall with Post-it notes, each detailing aspects of the customer's environment, skill level, values, motivations, relationships, usage patterns—anything the team could think of that described customers they might be interested in talking to.

Then they began to look at the notes to find groups, duplication, and patterns in the team's assumptions. It seemed that many people had an interest in talking to professional party planners. This wasn't a customer that PartyTime had targeted before, and it seemed reasonable to think that adding features for professionals could be lucrative for the company.

The next step was to formulate their assumptions about professional party planners into Customer hypotheses. One of the hypotheses they came up with was:

> We believe professional party planners are motivated to stay in constant contact with their clients when using a smartphone to organize an event.

By the time their first meeting was over, the team had nearly 20 Customer hypotheses like this, each with subtle variations on motivations (saving money, finding new clients, expanding their business offerings) and job-to-be-done (promoting their business, finding a venue, booking a caterer). These hypotheses served as the perfect guide to document the team's current thinking.

They also had the start of their Discussion Guide, with a list of questions they would ask party planners to validate their hypotheses. The team was excited to start talking with customers.

Susan scheduled customer visits with some local party planners and, after meeting with them and watching them interact with their clients, the team learned that many of their hypotheses had been invalidated. It turned out that most of the party planners they observed had advanced tools for scheduling, finding new clients, and expanding their businesses.

The tools that the planners were using were far more complex than PartyOrganizr. Many planners were communicating with their clients at their desk. Many were using a laptop and a desk phone rather than a smartphone.

This hypothesis had been invalidated, but they made an important discovery. The team learned that the needs of professional party planners didn't align with the simplicity of their mobile app.

It would've been interesting to expand PartyOrganizr to meet the advanced needs of professionals, but that strategy was just too ambitious for their small team. Thankfully, the team had plenty of time to quickly pivot off the segment of professional party planners.

They decided to turn their focus to customers who were actively using PartyOrganizr. The team defined "active" as any customer that had planned at least three parties in the past six months. They believed these customers would be great to have a conversation with because they were already using the product and may have needs the team hadn't considered. They quickly revised their hypotheses and made minor adjustments to their Discussion Guide.

Using their Twitter account, the team blasted a communication asking for active customers to help with a study they were running and even offered a gift certificate for participating. The tweet included a link to a short, five-question screener that helped the team determine whether a customer fit their definition of "active." Within hours, the team was getting responses and began scheduling calls with customers that met their profile.

After talking to this new set of customers, the team compiled all the notes from their interviews and printed them out.

Using the Customer playbook, the team completed a sensemaking exercise on their raw interview notes. A surprising finding was that many of the customers had talked about how they loved using the app to plan birthdays, graduations, and retirement parties, but one common complaint was that PartyOrganizr fell short when they tried to use it for planning potlucks.

In fact, many customers were managing their potlucks by using spreadsheets, email, and other workarounds for this missing functionality in PartyOrganizr. It was clear that they preferred to have PartyOrganizr help them organize their potluck party and stay in contact with party attendees.

The team conducted a quick competitive analysis and found that none of their competitors had specific features for planning potlucks. This seemed like an opportunity that could be a key differentiator for PartyOrganizr. They moved all the information they had on anything related to potlucks into their evidence file.

To do this right, the team needed to understand the problems customers faced when planning potlucks. They needed to determine if this was a problem worth solving.

Key Points

- To make great products, you must understand the entire story of the customers you serve. Formulating Customer hypotheses enables you to test the validity of your assumptions about your customers.

- It's important to segment your population. By defining detailed attributes about the type of customers you're targeting, you prevent generalizing your findings to other groups.

- A foundational parameter of the Customer hypothesis is the customer's motivation. The motivation helps you understand the customer's goal at a higher level, and separates the customer from the product or task they're engaged in.

- The [job-to-be-done] parameter of the Customer hypothesis is used to capture the job a customer "hires" to achieve a goal. Throughout the use of your product, customers will engage in a variety of tasks to achieve a desired outcome or goal. These tasks, or "jobs," are the factors you track so that you can separate the tasks customers do from your product.

Endnotes

1   [beren]
2   [un-carrier]
3   [epstein]
4   [meola]
5   [humble] p. 185
6   [alvarez] p. 27

[6]

The Problem

When Procter and Gamble (P&G) acquired Gillette, maker of razors and grooming products, P&G's president of men's grooming, Chip Bergh, became responsible for the new strategy. Although Gillette was already a successful company in the United States, Bergh was looking to leverage Gillette's existing capabilities while identifying new growth opportunities. As part of his growth strategy, he wanted to expand Gillette's business into new, emerging markets. This strategy led him to focus his attention on India.[1]

P&G, which is known for their customer-driven research, thought it would be best to take the entire team to India for two weeks. For the Gillette team, ethnographic research was a new practice; they'd built a very successful company using quantitative metrics to understand their customers. The idea of traveling all the way to India to learn more about customers seemed like a waste of resources. The Gillette team felt that they could easily gather the same insights from Indian men living in the United States, without having to incur the costs of a trip to India.

Even though he was met with resistance, Bergh was finally able to convince the team to go to India. During their visit, the team spent time observing the mundane routines and practices of men shaving throughout the week. While many of the practices were the same as those of American men, the team quickly learned that there was one fundamental difference: many of the men in India were shaving without the use of running water. In fact, most of the men filled a single cup of cold water to shave.

The team was mortified. It was difficult to watch these men struggle with their razors as they became clogged with hair, ultimately becoming ineffective and useless. To work properly, the Gillette razor technology required warm water to wash the blades clean. It had never occurred to the team that customers would be using their razors with cold water or without a large sink. Their entire line of razors did not perform well under those types of conditions. The team had never considered asking questions about water usage and availability, because running water was plentiful in the United States.

Excited that they had uncovered a new opportunity, in an emerging market, the team got to work on a new, single-blade razor specifically for markets without access to warm, running water.

Within three months, the Gillette Guard razor was released in India and became the best-selling razor on the market (Figure 6-1).[2]

FIGURE 6-1
The Guard razor
by Gillette

The story of Gillette is a powerful reminder of the cost of having the wrong assumptions about the problems our customers are facing. If the Gillette team had stayed in the United States and held onto their assumption that the challenges faced by American men would generalize to groups living outside of the United States, they may have never uncovered a unique opportunity for new customers in India.

The bottom line is that customers reward us for solving their problems and ignore us when we don't.

As with the type of customer and their motivations, we're susceptible to having incorrect assumptions about the customer's problem as well. If we don't validate that our customers are, in fact, having a problem and that it's painful enough for them to seek a resolution, we end up building solutions in search of a problem.

Focusing on Customers' Limitations

At its heart, the Problem stage is where we focus on what's preventing the customers from achieving their goals. As in the Customer stage, we want to gain a full picture of the problem space; only then can we provide the proper solution. Misunderstanding the problem can lead us down a path of providing ineffective solutions, or worse, introducing new problems our customers didn't have before. While we may have technical limitations within our product, there can also be many external factors that prevent our customers from achieving a desirable outcome.

Let's return to our example website that helps customers find service providers in their area. There could be many factors that prevent our customers from successfully finding a provider:

Money

Customers are limited by the amount they can spend on services like house cleaning, childcare, and pool cleaning. Therefore, finding a service provider that is affordable is of high importance.

Time

Perhaps the customer doesn't have a lot of time to spend looking for the right service provider. They may visit our site with an expectation of finding providers quickly, but leave in frustration because it takes too much time to filter results to find the provider they're looking for.

Knowledge

Our customers could have a diverse set of knowledge and experience. Some might find the site too basic and would prefer advanced features, while others want an experience tailored to someone just getting started.

Confidence

Customers can put off decisions or lose motivation if they feel anxious or defeated. Great products engender trust and empower customers, giving them the confidence they need to achieve their goals.

Customers may have expertise with service providers and confidence they can navigate the web, but have limited skills when typing long messages on a keyboard. In this case, these customers may love the website, but find the process of completing contact forms for service providers daunting and laborious.

How to Identify Customers' Problems

Many of you may be saying, "We talk to our customers all the time, and when we ask them about what frustrates them, they say they're 'okay' or they ask for something we can't fix."

As you begin your investigation, talking with customers and lifting every rock, your team may become frustrated by the lack of valuable leads. While talking with customers is a great way to explore your customers' problems, it can be difficult to identify problems your team can actually solve.

As an interviewer, it's critically important to not only listen to what the customer is telling you, but also look for what they're *not* telling you. Sometimes customers want to be agreeable and not come off as rude or complaining. They may accept a problem or inefficient workaround because it's "not that big of a deal." Without careful observation or attentive listening, you might overlook these types of problems.

Let's look at another example from Procter & Gamble. In 1994, P&G partnered with Continuum, a research and design firm, to help them identify new innovations in the category of home cleaning with the goal of generating $5 billion in revenue from new product lines.[3]

If we talked to customers about how they clean their floors, we imagine that many of them would say they use a broom and a mop, and that for the most part, that method is "okay."

To get around this, Continuum decided to not only talk with customers, but also to visit them at home and watch them clean their floors. A case study on Continuum's website explains what they learned:[4]

> Mopping floors is a dirty job. It's also tedious and time-consuming. During our visits, we watched people engaging in a largely unpleasant experience—one that involved direct contact with dirt and water and took far longer than it should have. People changed into old clothes beforehand, in anticipation of the messy task

ahead. Then they swept the floors with a broom and dustpan. And once they finally got to work with their mop buckets, people spent just as much time and effort wringing out their mops as they did cleaning the floors.

The team realized that the complete process of cleaning floors was problematic. It wasn't any one single product that was creating friction, but rather the process itself. What they observed, time and again, was that mopping floors was tedious and unnecessarily time-consuming.

So, the design team decided to look for ways they could reinvent the way people mop. Watching how mops pushed dirt around and noting the fact that customers had to sweep before they mopped, the team began to wonder, "What if a mop could *attract* dirt to itself?"

The team began looking at a process where disposable pads could be charged, electrostatically, to attract dirt while customers ran it across their floors. The product eventually became known as the Swiffer and was an astronomical success for P&G (Figure 6-2). In fact, by 2004, the Swiffer was in 25% of households and *Businessweek* listed it as one of its "20 Products That Shook the Stock Market."[5]

FIGURE 6-2

The Swiffer Sweeper

There's incredible power in identifying problems through customer behavior. These problems are often undiscovered because it's part of the customer's typical routine; they aren't expressing them as problems since they've become accustomed to the limitation.

It may not be possible to travel to India or visit customers in their homes, but that doesn't mean you can't ask customers questions that help elicit their behavior.

Returning to our example website, if we were interested in understanding how customers behave when searching for providers on the site, we might ask questions like:

- In the past six months, how often would you say you've searched for a provider on our website?

- Was there ever a time you couldn't find a provider? What did you do?

- When you locate a provider that you're interested in talking with, how do you contact them?

- If a service provider hadn't called you back in 24 hours, what would you do?

From a purely scientific approach, relying on the customer's memory or their ability to predict their behavior is less than ideal. However, responses to these types of questions can still be a useful indicator of their behavior. In short, direct observation is always best, but if you don't have the time or budget, these types of questions can be helpful too.

Formulating a Problem Hypothesis

As in the Customer stage, before we talk with customers we want to formulate our assumptions about our customers' problems into hypotheses that can be validated. The Problem stage of the HPF uses the following hypothesis template:

> We believe [type of customers] are frustrated by [job-to-be-done] because of [problem].

In previous chapters, we've discussed the [type of customers] and [job-to-be-done] parameters. The Problem stage introduces the [problem] parameter, which essentially is the problem or limitation you believe exists for the customer when they engage in the [job-to-be-done].

Let's go back to the Customer hypotheses we created for StarDoc, the desktop publishing software:

> We believe office administrators working for small businesses are motivated to promote their business offerings when creating promotional brochures.

Ideally, at the Problem stage, we have validated that this statement is true. In other words, we talked to office administrators working for small businesses, and determined that many of them use promotional brochures to promote their business offerings.

If we discovered that many office administrators were using StarDoc to create promotional brochures, we would want to know of any limitations that prevent them from achieving that goal.

This leads us to the following Problem hypothesis template:

> We believe office administrators working for small businesses are frustrated when creating promotional brochures because of [problem].

We've taken the type of customer (office administrators working for small businesses) and job-to-be-done (creating promotional brochures), and *progressed* them to the Problem stage. This is where the *Progression* comes from in the Hypothesis Progression Framework.

As a team, we can now list limitations, constraints, problems, or frustrations that get in the way of office administrators successfully creating product brochures.

For example, maybe we believe that, when office administrators create promotional brochures, they are frustrated by:

- The lack of aesthetically pleasing designs
- The time it takes to get started
- Having to print the brochure correctly, so it can be folded the right way
- Resizing images in the brochure and ensuring that they are still of premium print quality

Therefore, if we wanted talk to customers about these problems, our Discussion Guide might look like this:

- How do you feel about the design choices StarDoc gives you for creating a brochure?

- About how long did it take you to get started with creating your brochure?

- Talk to me about the process of printing the brochure.

- How do you go about adding images to your brochure? What's that process like for you?

Of course, we could have many more questions in our Discussion Guide.

One question that really opens up an interview is what Cindy Alvarez calls the "magic wand question."[6] We could use it in our interview like this:

> If you could wave a magic wand and change anything—doesn't matter if it's possible or not—about creating promotional brochures, what would it be?

Giving the customer a "magic wand" to point at the job-to-be-done allows them the creative freedom to explore their dream scenario. Customers may come up with some silly and unrealistic answers, but many times, you'll find meaningful insights when you let them imagine a delightful experience.

Avoiding Problems *Not* Worth Solving

When talking with customers, it's important to not only listen for problems that are worth solving, but problems that *aren't* worth solving as well.

Going back to our service provider website example, imagine we believed our service providers were frustrated because they didn't have a website to promote their services. We believed there might be a service opportunity for us to help our providers build their own websites and host them within our portal.

When we talked to our providers who didn't have a website, we heard many frustrations. They complained about not having an online presence and how they wished creating a website could be easier for their business. They were frustrated because many of their competitors had websites, and they felt like it was a competitive advantage. In fact, some providers even suggested we offer a website creation service. One provider said, "I'll give you my wallet!" if we solved this problem for him.

This may seem like a problem worth solving. However, the desire to have a website is not the same as having a *problem* with not having a website.

Imagine we had asked them questions like:

- How are you getting around this problem today?

- How often do you try to solve this problem?

- How much time do you typically spend investigating solutions to this problem?

- How much money have you invested to try to solve this problem?

Many of our service providers said we should help them build their website, but when we asked them how they were currently addressing this problem, their responses were less than encouraging.

For example, none of the providers we spoke to had spent any money to solve this problem (even the one who said he'd give us his wallet). Additionally, only a few had spent time investigating a solution. Many admitted that they hadn't really thought about it until we brought it up.

Therefore, we might conclude that while providers are frustrated about not having a website, it simply isn't a problem they're motivated to solve.

So, we need to ask ourselves, "If customers aren't willing to buy other products that solve this problem, what makes us think they'd be willing to buy *our solution?*"

As you explore customer motivations and problems, it will become increasingly important to collect and organize your findings. As we discussed in Chapter 4, there are many digital tools that can help you organize documents and notes.

We also find there is tremendous value in meeting as a team, periodically throughout the project, to reflect on and assess how your customer interviews are going. Teams that have a constant, ongoing dialog about what they're learning tend to grow much more rapidly in their understanding of the customer and their problems.

Be sure to check out the Customer and Problem playbooks at the back of this book. We've included sensemaking activities that can help you "flatten out" your customer interview data. This will help you see all the data points that have been collected, so you and your team can begin to identify patterns.

We will repeat this process, iterating and attempting to validate our Customer and Problem hypotheses, until we've gained a high degree of confidence that we understand the customer and their problems. Throughout the first two stages of the HPF, Customer and Problem, we are developing our understanding of the customer. However, customer development is only half the equation. Discovering a unique opportunity or a worthy problem to solve can be exciting, but how we *solve* that problem will ultimately determine our success.

Key Points

- Fully understanding your customers' problems can unlock new opportunities for your products.

- Lack of money, resources, knowledge, confidence, or skill can prevent customers from achieving their goals.

- While talking to customers is a great, low-cost way to capture rich customer data, direct observation of customer behavior can unlock insights that customers don't mention, because they think they're not interesting or unimportant. If possible, try to observe customers engaging in the activities you're interested in.

- Sometimes customers can be quite vocal when they request a product or feature to solve a problem, but you shouldn't mistake their requests as a tacit agreement that they are willing to *pay for a solution*.

PartyTime Apps Revisited

Armed with several validated Customer hypotheses, the team was feeling more confident about their understanding of active customers who use smartphones to plan events. The team was getting really excited about the potluck opportunity, but they had been here before only to realize that customers weren't all that invested in solving the problem.

They had to increase their confidence that customers were frustrated with the process of planning potluck parties and explore what limitations were causing the frustration.

As in the previous week, the team had plenty of assumptions about what might prevent a customer from successfully planning a potluck. The team began to formulate their assumptions into Problem hypotheses:

> We believe potluck party planners are frustrated by organizing potlucks because guests often bring the same dish to the party.

This revised hypothesis made it easy to create a Discussion Guide so that the team would be able to ask the right questions.

Rather than source their own customers, they decided to recruit *anyone* that owned a smartphone and had organized at least two potlucks within the last six months.

The team had fallen into a smooth cadence and, within a week, had talked to nearly 40 customers who had either attended or organized a potluck. Many of the team's problem hypotheses were validated. It seemed that their assumptions around what was frustrating customers about organizing potlucks were correct. That was a big confidence booster for the team!

Additionally, it seemed that customers were trying many methods to solve the problem—everything from posting paper sign-up sheets to tracking dishes over email, and, in one customer's case, even purchasing three different mobile apps to organize a potluck. Customers seemed to unanimously agree: none of these methods worked very well.

The energy on the team was electric. They had found a promising opportunity! Now all they had to do was figure out the right way to solve it.

Endnotes

1 [lafley] pp. 107–118
2 [lafley] pp. 110–111
3 [continuum]
4 [continuum]
5 [lafley] pp. 66–67
6 [alvarez] p. 98

[7]

The Concept

In 1950, the United States Air Force had a mission-critical problem. Pilots were having trouble controlling their aircraft and, thus, crashes and deaths were on the rise.[1]

The Air Force was a relatively new military expansion and the country was teetering on the edge of war with Korea. Now was not the time for officials to start losing confidence in their pilots' ability to fly newer aircraft.

So teams set out to discover the problem. Engineers ran tests on the planes, instructors reviewed their training programs, and investigators considered the possibility of pilot error. However, these factors did not appear to have a significant effect on the planes that had crashed.

It was then that the Air Force considered the experience of the cockpit itself.

Over two decades earlier, the Army had designed the first cockpit based on the average pilot's height, weight, arm length, and other physical dimensions (see Figure 7-1). The size and shape of the seat, the distance to the pedals and stick, the height of the windshield, and even the shape of the helmets were all built using these averaged measurements.[2]

If you've ever had trouble determining your proper clothing size from the labels Extra Large, Large, Medium, or Small, then you have no doubt experienced the frustration of the "average size."

It occurred to the Air Force that perhaps the cockpit of their aircraft was too small. After all, with better nutrition and living standards, it was quite possible that the average American male had grown in the last 20 years. (Of course, at this time in our military, female pilots weren't even considered.)

FIGURE 7-1

Even though there had
been many advances in
aviation, the Air Force
was still designing
cockpits based on
much earlier planes,
like the US Army's
Curtiss A-3 Falcon
(1925)

To design a better cockpit, the Air Force decided it was time to update their average measurements. Researchers at Wright-Patterson Air Force Base in Ohio began creating new measurements from more than 4,000 pilots. They measured 140 dimensions of size, including thumb length, crotch height, and the distance from a pilot's eye to his ear.[3]

A 23-year-old researcher named Gilbert S. Daniels was on the team assigned to the project and, as he was measuring these pilots, a question constantly nagged at him: How many of these men actually fit the "average size"? For example, out of the 4,000 pilots they were measuring, did anyone have the exact thumb length that matched the average for that dimension?

So Daniels looked at all the measurements the team had so far. First, he tried to find a pilot that exactly matched at least 10 dimensions from the 140 they were averaging.

He found no one matched at least 10 dimensions.

Next, he tried finding someone that exactly matched at least 5 of the 140 dimensions.

Again, not a single pilot matched at least 5 dimensions.

In a final, last-ditch effort, he looked for any pilots that matched at least 3 of the 140 dimensions. Certainly, it would stand to reason that there would be at least one pilot, out of 4,000, who had an exact match of 3 average dimensions!

He found none.

In his 1952 report, "The Average Man," Daniels concluded:[4]

> The "average man" is a misleading and illusory concept as a basis for design criteria, and is particularly so when more than one dimension is being considered.

Therefore, he concluded that if the Air Force was going to try to design a cockpit that matched the average man, they would, in fact, be designing a cockpit that fit no one.

The Air Force hadn't considered looking at the problem this way. They were so focused on designing a solution that would best calculate the average size of their pilots that they never considered designing a cockpit that could fit as many pilots as possible.

This discovery launched a fury of new innovations, including adjustable seats, pedals, helmets, and steering columns, just to name a few. Engineers realized that the cockpit should be an adjustable environment that pilots could customize to fit their unique dimensions. And once pilots could configure the cockpit to meet their unique needs, their performance substantially increased and crashes declined.

Adjustable cockpits also had an unintended benefit. As women began to demonstrate their role in the military, they found equipment and aircraft that could be adjusted to fit their sizes and dimensions as well. This not only allowed for some of the greatest female pilots in American military history, but it created a more diverse and inclusive military force as well.

The Power of Problem Framing

If I had an hour to solve a problem, I'd spend 55 minutes thinking about the problem and 5 minutes solving it.
—ALBERT EINSTEIN

If Gilbert Daniels had simply followed orders and tried to build a better calculation, the Air Force would have continued down a path of building a cockpit that didn't work well for anyone. However, he questioned the conventional wisdom. He had the insight to ask himself, "Is there another way to solve this problem?"

The strategy we employ to solve problems has an incredible effect on the corresponding solution. If our problem focus is too narrow, we miss the greater issues at play. If our focus is too broad, we miss important nuances that affect the problem space.

Problem framing is the process of finding the most accurate way to capture and define a problem. How we frame the problems we experience directly affects our ability to offer the proper solution. Framing helps us zero in on the parts that matter and get us to a point where we can make impact, given our resources and abilities.

For example, say we're a small team of five people and we want to solve the problem of climate change. Now, that's a big, very complex problem. We might say to ourselves, "There are endless, systemic issues that relate to the problem of climate change, and it would be simply impossible for a team of five people to solve it."

This, of course, frames the problem too broadly. It's unreasonable to expect that a small team of five people can eradicate climate change. But what if they frame the problem a bit differently? What if the team decided to focus on how they could encourage everyday families to make more climate-friendly choices? Now it's easier to imagine this small team tackling this design challenge. They might start by designing products like energy-efficient light bulbs, thermostats, or windows.

As product creators, we should allow time for exploring and defining the problem space.

Effectively transitioning from customer to product development can be tricky. That's why we've added a Concept stage to the HPF. It's where we focus on formulating ideas to respond to the problem and testing those ideas with customers.

Formulating Ideas

The most creative teams maintain a supportive environment and space to explore ideas and share them without fear of judgment.

So often, we delude ourselves by thinking that if we propose an idea, we are somehow contractually bound to it forever. What we forget is that ideas are cheap; they cost us very little. They can be easily refined or discarded. Building the wrong thing, however, is incredibly expensive.

Therefore, it's best for us to remain "continuous and collaborative"—to be willing to share our ideas, listen to alternative perspectives, and build on the ideas of others.

Tom and David Kelly, founders of the world-class design agency IDEO, believe that continuous collaboration is a core component to creative exploration:[5]

> At IDEO, we seldom say, "That's a bad idea" or "That won't work" or "We've tried that before." When we disagree with someone else's idea, we push ourselves to ask, "What would make it better? What can I add to make it a great idea?" Or, "What new idea does that spur?" By doing so, we keep creative momentum going instead of cutting off the flow of ideas. Throwing cold water on one person's contribution can bring conversation to a halt; it is the back and forth of ideas that can lead you to new and unexpected places.

How we approach the problem can affect our ability to generate ideas.

Dr. Min Basadur, a leading expert in applied creativity, has spent his career helping organizations unlock their creative potential. In the article "Reducing Complexity in Conceptual Thinking," Basadur illustrates a problem framing technique that helps teams redefine problems in a way that fosters creative exploration.[6] It starts with a fundamental question: "How might we?"

How

Opens the door for new questions and curiosity. It suggests that there may be a new way of looking at the problem.

Might

Suggests there may be many ways to solve this problem. Some may work and others may not. For now, we simply ask ourselves what *might* work. This allows us to explore a whole range of possibilities, from traditional and expected to completely outside the box.

We

Solving complex problems requires the work of many, not one. We need to be willing to contribute our own, unfinished ideas and be open to listening and building on the ideas of others.

While "How might we?" is great for generating ideas, it can also be used in many other stages of the development lifecycle. We've used it on smaller, internal challenges (e.g., "How might we recruit more customers for this study?") or broad, strategic, business challenges (e.g., "How might we attract college students to our products?").

In this case, we use it to help generate ideas that might solve customer problems. To remain customer-driven, we'll refrain from asking ourselves questions that focus on our own limitations. For example, we shouldn't ask, "Why can't we?" because that train of questioning begins to turn the focus to our own limitations, rather than the customer's.

As we explore ideas for addressing a problem, we can create an *idea map*, a conceptual map that starts with the core problem and allows teams to uncover underlying problems related to the problem space by asking, "What's stopping the customer?" and "What else?" (Figure 7-2).

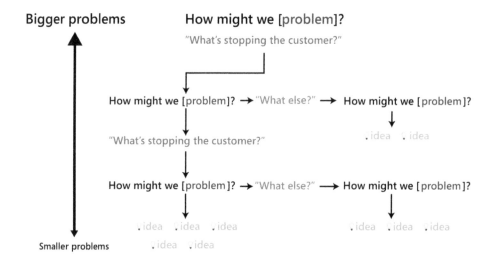

FIGURE 7-2
Using "How might we?" to generate an idea map

Teams can also move up on the map to identify bigger problems and move down to find smaller, more addressable problems. Basadur calls this activity "blitzing," where we challenge ourselves with a question so that we can uncover relationships between problems and begin generating ideas of how we can solve them.[7]

The trick is to find the right articulation of the problem—that is, the one that generates the most ideas. Most often, this happens organically. Some teams will start with a broad problem (e.g., "How might we solve the crisis of climate change?") and work their way down to something more manageable (e.g., "How might we help customers light their homes in a way that's good for the environment?). Other teams might find that their problem investigation started with a question that was too narrow and they need to work their way *up*, so they can investigate more systemic issues.

How to Pick the Best Potential Opportunity

Once your team has generated a list of possible ideas, it can be hard to know which idea presents the greatest opportunity. Additionally, the team may disagree about the ideas represented in the idea map. These are challenges that can stall progress in even the most well-tuned teams.

Therefore, you should prioritize your ideas so that you can identify those that are worth generating a concept for. Here are some pivots to help you do so:

Cost

Depending on your resource availability, you may decide to prioritize your ideas based on their estimated development cost. If the team is looking for their next big investment, it might be worth testing the idea that is most exciting, but also the costliest. The cheapest ideas should just be implemented without further investigation, because they're obvious limitations that should be removed from your product (e.g., software bugs).

Risk

You can prioritize your ideas based on product risk. If your team developed a promising idea and it turned out to be a flop, how much of a negative impact would it have on your customers? Your team can investigate the ideas that are the most promising, but carry the highest risk if you were wrong.

Customer impact

Based on your ongoing communication with customers, you can organize ideas around what you believe will have the most impact on, or generate the highest satisfaction from, your customers. Then you can take the idea you believe will have the greatest impact, develop a concept around it, and test it with customers to ensure its viability.

Differentiation

You can organize your ideas based on their uniqueness compared to solutions provided by your competitors. The most differentiated ideas may be the ones worth pursuing. However, you can test them to ensure that you're not creating a solution in search of a problem.

Business goals

Your organization may have an overarching business goal, such as entering a new market, getting customers to upgrade to the latest version, or encouraging in-app purchasing. You can prioritize the ideas that you believe will best align with your organization's business goals. At this stage, you might be making your best guess, but that's okay. You can always validate the idea with customers, against these business goals, as you refine the idea into a concept.

As a team, you'll need to decide what projects have the greatest return. One decision-making exercise we've found useful is to organize your ideas into an Impact/Effort Matrix (Figure 7-3).[8]

FIGURE 7-3
The Impact/Effort
Matrix

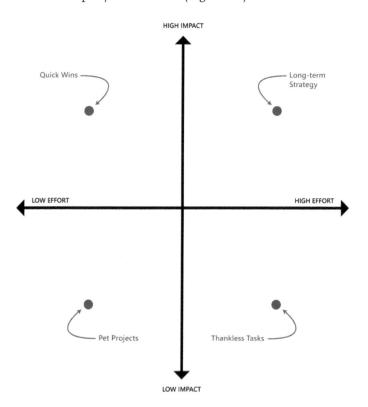

Essentially, you organize your ideas into a 2×2 matrix, comparing the impact on customers with the effort for the team. In terms of direct impact on customers, the ideas that have a higher impact are projects that the team believes will improve customer value, satisfaction, desirability, or usefulness. When your ideas are organized on the matrix, the team can assess them based on the following criteria:

High Impact/Low Effort ("Quick Wins")

Ideas that have a high impact on the customer, but require a little amount of work, should be obvious wins. These are projects that are low-hanging fruit, so you should just plan to make these changes.

High Impact/High Effort ("Long-term Strategy")

These are ideas that could have a tremendous impact on customers, but they'll require a significant investment from your team. These ideas won't materialize overnight, so you'll have to be strategic and create a long-term plan to bring them to fruition.

Low Impact/Low Effort ("Pet Projects")

These ideas have little direct impact on customers, but don't cost that much in terms of time invested or resources. These might be personal projects or fixes that are a sort of "spring cleaning"—things that need to be done but probably don't justify the team's entire focus.

Low Impact/High Effort ("Thankless Tasks")

These are projects that will require a significant investment, but won't likely produce any immediate or direct benefit for the customer. These could be underlying platform changes to software code or a restructuring of tools and processes to make the team more efficient. Like pet projects, these tasks can be hard for the team to justify, but they could lead to critical issues down the road.

Formulating a Concept Hypothesis

In the beginning of transitioning your idea to concept, it's important to reflect on your intent for the concept: what problem you're planning to solve, who would use it, and how you'll know that the concept is effective in meeting your customers' goals.

Just like the Customer and Problem stages, the Concept stage has a hypothesis template that allows us to track these types of parameters:

> We believe [concept] will solve [problem] and be valuable for [type of customer] when doing [job-to-be-done].
>
> We will know this to be true when we see [criteria].

As we've discussed in previous chapters, the parameters from the Customer and Problem stages progress to the Concept stage. However, we've introduced two new parameters:

[concept]

This is the concept we believe will not only solve the problem, but do it in a way that customers find valuable.

[criteria]

This parameter represents the measurable criteria we'll use to determine if the Concept is providing value for the customer.

To see how "How might we?" and Concept hypotheses work, let's revisit PartyTime Apps.

PartyTime Apps Revisited

The team decided to frame the problem by asking, "How might we make it easier for customers to organize a potluck?"

Then they began asking themselves, "What's stopping the customer?" and all the frustrations that customers talked about during their interviews began to pour out:

- It's frustrating when people bring similar dishes.
- It's hard to find a dish that everyone will like.
- When you change your mind about what you want to bring, it's a pain to let everyone know.
- Preparing a dish to feed a lot of people can be expensive.
- If you have strict dietary needs, it can be hard to know what dishes are okay to eat.

Now that they had many of the problems identified, they rephrased each problem using the "How might we?" language:

- How might we prevent customers from bringing similar dishes?
- How might we help customers decide what dish they should bring to the potluck?
- How might we help customers update party guests when they've changed their mind about the dish they want to bring?
- How might we help customers prepare dishes that are delicious but inexpensive?
- How might we help customers avoid dishes that don't meet their dietary needs?

The team began to excitedly brainstorm all sorts of ways the PartyOrganizr app could help solve these problems.

Finally, the team prioritized their ideas using the Impact/Effort Matrix. This allowed them to visualize the customer impact of each idea and its associated development effort.

The team was now able to identify the ideas that would have the most impact on customers. They also identified some "low-hanging fruit" opportunities that engineering could begin to address immediately.

Finally, the team began to rally around the idea of creating a "Potluck Planner Pack," an add-on that customers could purchase through the app store and add to their PartyOrganizr app.

They had the following Concept hypothesis:

> We believe the Potluck Planner Pack will solve the difficulty of organizing potlucks and be valuable for potluck party planners when organizing potlucks.

But how would they know that this hypothesis was validated? What sort of criteria would make them agree that this concept solves the problem in a way that's valuable for customers?

They added the following criteria to their Concept hypothesis:

> We believe the Potluck Planner Pack will solve the difficulty of organizing potlucks and be valuable for potluck party planners when organizing potlucks.
>
> We will know this to be true when we see customers give a score of at least 4 out of 5 on "intent to use" and "need fulfillment."

To summarize, the PartyTime Apps team believed the following parameters of their Concept hypothesis to be true:

Concept

A Potluck Planner Pack add-on that adds a set of features to PartyOrganizr, specifically designed for organizing a potluck.

Problem

There may be other problems that the Potluck Planner Pack could solve, but for this concept to be viable, it must *at least* solve the problem of organizing potlucks. If it can't do that, this concept won't be going very far.

Criteria

In this case, they had high expectations that this concept solved the problem in a way that customers would find valuable. Therefore, they expected customers to rate their "intent to use" and "need fulfillment" at least a 4 out of 5.

Plotting Events Using a Storyboard

Your concept is not just a collection of features; it's an experience, derived from multiple touch points. Storyboarding can be an effective tool to help illustrate the experience a customer will have with your concept.

The story of your concept can take shape over each frame of the storyboard. We like to start with a three-frame storyboard that shows the "broad strokes" of the experience. These three frames can show the story of the customer before your concept is introduced, during, and after (Figure 7-4).

FIGURE 7-4
You can use a three-frame storyboard to show the experience of your concept before, during, and after it's introduced

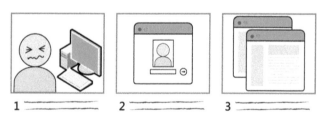

Underneath each frame, it's a good idea to write a sentence or two to describe what it represents.

When starting your storyboards, here are some things you could consider:

- What is the motivation of the customer? What are they trying to achieve in your story? ([motivation])

- What task is the customer is engaged in? ([job-to-be-done])

- What's preventing the customer from achieving their goal? ([problem]) How does it make the customer feel?

- What solution is introduced to help the customer overcome their limitations? ([concept])

You can show these storyboards to customers to get feedback on their accuracy. You can ask customers questions like: "Does this story resonate with you? Is this something you're familiar with? Have you ever experienced anything like this story?"

Testing Your Concepts with Customers

During the holiday season in 1975, Sony released a device that, they believed, would change American households forever. They suggested it was as important as the invention of the telephone and told their customers it would allow them to "break the time barrier."[9]

Sony called it the LV-901, but most came to know it as the Betamax (Figure 7-5).

The device debuted in retail stores at a hefty price tag of $2,295.[10] While the Betamax was heavy and bulky, Sony still claimed that it was a state-of-the-art design. It included a cassette recorder that consumers had never seen before, an analog clock, and a 19-inch, full-color Trinitron display.

Betamax was the first in-home video cassette recorder (VCR). While it had many features, its chief selling point was the fact that customers could finally record television shows. With today's DVR, on-demand, and online streaming services, it's inconceivable that we would miss our favorite television program, but in the 70s it was a problem for many television watchers.

A year later, JVC, makers of a similar video recording concept, introduced their format of tape and video recorders, which they called VHS (Video Home System). Thus began the entrenched rivalry of the "video format war."[11]

FIGURE 7-5
The Sony LV-901,
commonly known as
the Betamax

For the time, this was a rivalry on par with Mac versus PC or iPhone versus Android. Anyone who followed video formats had an opinion about which recording format was better, and heated debates over the topic weren't uncommon.

When JVC entered the market, Sony already had a commanding position. Sony had a video format that was widely considered superior in quality and durability, and their brand was emerging as a strong player in American consumer electronics. Even with all this wind in their sails, however, Betamax was a complete failure and JVC's VHS format beat them in a landslide.

How did this happen?

There was no question that consumers wanted the ability to record their television programs at home. For all intents and purposes, we can agree that the problem hypothesis had been clearly validated. However, Sony and JVC had fundamentally different approaches to solving the problem. Conceptually, Sony valued quality, precision, and design, whereas JVC focused on affordability and availability.

One of the critical differences between Betamax and VHS was the amount of recording time. Betamax cassettes were substantially smaller than VHS cassettes, so they were more limited in the amount of tape they could hold. Betamax tapes could record only an hour of programming, whereas VHS tapes could record up to four hours. Sony believed that, because most television shows were less than an hour, the lower recording time was a worthwhile tradeoff for better-quality video recording.[12] JVC, on the other hand, was willing to accept lesser-quality recording to ensure that their cassettes were inexpensive.

Soon, small businesses were popping up to rent movies to customers so they could watch them at home. Many customers at this point couldn't afford their own VCR, so they would often rent one along with the movie they wanted to watch.

These business owners had to decide which format they wanted to carry in their stores because it became too costly to buy every movie in two formats. Because the VHS format was cheaper and the players were more readily available, it slowly became the standard for home movie rentals.

In other words, the availability of VHS in rental stores helped JVC's format quickly become the standard that consumers associated with home video entertainment.

At the end of the day, Sony was solving the right problem ("I want to record my favorite TV show and watch movies at home") and they were also first to market. However, they were unsuccessful in solving the problem in a way customers found valuable. Sony focused their efforts on creating a product that had superior video and audio quality. While this might have been important to some consumers, most customers wanted affordable tapes and VCR players. In short, customers weren't willing to pay the premium for superior quality.

If Sony had asked customers, "Would you like to have superior audio and video quality when recording programs?" they would have undoubtedly said yes. However, if Sony had asked customers, "How important is quality compared to the price of the VCR or the amount you can record on single tape?" customers may have been willing to trade quality for other benefits. That would've been an important discovery for Sony as they began to prioritize the development of Betamax.

By testing the benefits and limitations of your concept, you'll determine the minimum number of features to include in your solution while still delivering value to your customer. This cost-benefit tradeoff is what leads you to your minimum viable product (MVP).

The Concept Value Test

The approach we use to test our concepts with customers and get their feedback is called the Concept Value Test (CVT). Customers can evaluate your early thinking, give you feedback, and help you assess whether you're presenting enough value with your concept. Let's look at the components of the CVT and how they work.

Unique Value Proposition

Every concept should propose a unique idea, or value proposition. In the business world, you might refer to this as your "elevator pitch." Essentially, you're describing to the customer, as clearly and succinctly as possible, how your concept is unique and worth paying attention to.[13]

After revealing your concept's value proposition, you can ask customers, "How do you feel about this?" or "If something like this was available to you, how might you use it?" You can also show them a storyboard that walks through a few of the high-level touch points of the experience. The trick is to provide just enough detail so the customer "gets it," without going into too many specifics. Keeping your value proposition or storyboards a little bit vague allows the customer to fill in the experience with their own preconceived notions.

For example, imagine we're going to offer a website creation service for our service providers on our website portal. Our value proposition might sound like this:

> The Provider Pro Plus service helps you create your own business website. Provider Pro Plus gives you access to hundreds of ready-made website templates; they're easy to configure and look fantastic. All the templates are hosted on our servers and have a guaranteed uptime of 99.9%.

This description generates a lot of questions: "What would it cost? What do the templates look like? What options can I configure in the templates? What does 99.9% uptime mean?" This is intentional. We want to hear the types of questions the customer asks because those are the questions that we'll need to answer when/if we release this solution. If a customer does ask a question about implementation, you can always turn it back to them (e.g., "What options would *you* expect to configure in the templates?").

Allowing customers to fill in the blanks is a valuable exercise. It helps you validate your assumptions or highlight parts of the experience you may have overlooked.

Benefits

Each concept has a series of benefits. The benefits should not focus on specific implementation details but rather on the *value* the customer will receive by using your concept.

In the case of Provider Pro Plus service, the benefits would be all the feature ideas that we generated during our "How might we?" brainstorm.

The Provider Pro Plus will:

- Allow you to configure a website in just three easy steps.
- Automatically pull your business details from your profile, and put them into a stylized web template.
- Track visitors to your site and email you a weekly "activity report."
- Provide a "Contact Us" form. Submissions get sent to your email address.

You can introduce these benefits in short (one- or two-sentence) descriptions. Much like the overall unique value proposition, we're interested in the customer's perceptions of what these benefits mean to them. We're interested in their questions because those will highlight the things they care about. For example:

Customer: "Does the activity report include pages they actually visit on my site?"

Interviewer: "Is that something you would need? How would that be helpful to you?"

Customer: "Well, yeah...My shop has a bunch of automobile detailing and repair services we provide, so I guess I'd want to know which services people visited the most."

You can also have the customer rank the benefits in order, from "most impactful" to "least impactful." This helps the team prioritize the benefits of the concept and establish where the cutline is for their MVP. By asking the customer to rank the benefits, you're able to see what's most valuable and what's less valuable to them.

Limitations

Even the best concepts have limitations. The team should reflect not only on the things that the concept will do, but also what it *won't* do. It's important to be honest and transparent about your concept's limitations. It's better to learn what limitations will prevent customers from using your concept before you start building it.

You can reveal your limitations much like you revealed your benefits, in one- or two-sentence descriptions.

The Provider Pro Plus will *not* allow you to:

- Modify source code or change underlying CSS files.
- Host files over 100 MB in size.
- Export data collected from online forms.
- Provide administrative access to other users.

As with the benefits, you'll also have the customer rank limitations in order of "most impactful" to "least impactful." This will help you identify the biggest barriers preventing customers from using your concept.

Note, however, that what you think is a dealbreaker limitation may not be a limitation at all. For example, imagine that our service providers liked the idea that they couldn't modify the source code of their websites. They felt that if we provided tools to manage code, it would make the experience too intimidated and confusing. They actually liked that we were hiding the code from them and saw it as a benefit.

This understanding would save our team *countless* hours because we would avoid investing in features that customers won't use. Imagine how much effort we might have wasted building tools for providers to modify source code, only to find out later that no one used them.

These types of discoveries are what make CVTs so valuable.

Ratings

During the CVT, we will get rich, qualitative responses from our customers about the concept we're presenting, but we'll want to collect quantitative data as well. Since we typically work with small sample sizes for CVT, we consider these "soft quant" measures. We're not looking for statistical significance in our findings; we just want to determine if we've "moved the needle" with our concept. As the concept evolves, we'll be able to monitor and compare customers' ratings to judge the effectiveness of our iterations.

After we walk customers through the concept's value proposition, benefits, and limitations, we ask them the following questions.

WOULD THIS CONCEPT SOLVE A PROBLEM OR FULFILL A NEED FOR YOU?

1	2	3	4	5

Definitely would not   Definitely would

WHY TO ASK THIS. When talking with customers about your concept, you have an opportunity to continue validating your Problem hypothesis. In other words, you should always check that you're solving the right problem.

WHAT TO LISTEN FOR. Listen for responses like:

- "I don't have this problem, but I know a lot of other people who do."

- "I don't have this problem, but this is still a great idea."

If you're hearing this sort of sentiment from many customers, it may be an indication that your concept isn't solving the right problem for this type of customer. You may consider revising your customer segment or choosing to focus on solving a different problem.

ASSUMING THIS CONCEPT WAS AVAILABLE TODAY, WOULD YOU TRY IT?

1	2	3	4	5

Definitely would not   Definitely would

WHY TO ASK THIS. This question helps you determine how willing the customer is to try this concept. If the customer is frustrated with the problem you're trying to solve and thinks your concept solves it, then you should expect a high rating.

WHAT TO LISTEN FOR. Listen for red flag responses like:

- "I don't have this problem right now, but if I did, I'd definitely try this."

- "I don't have time right now, but when I get some free time, I'd be willing to check out your concept."

These are indications that you're solving a problem, but not a problem that customers are experiencing *right now*. Additionally, they may be an indication that the problem you're trying to solve is simply not an urgent one.

Put simply: if customers are not motivated to solve the problem, it's likely that they don't need your concept.

HOW LIKELY IS IT THAT YOU WOULD RECOMMEND THIS CONCEPT TO A FRIEND, FAMILY MEMBER, OR COLLEAGUE?

1	2	3	4	5

Definitely would not   Definitely would

WHY TO ASK THIS. When you ask a customer what they think of your concept, they may give you a positive response; but ask them to put their reputation on the line, and they become much more critical. We affectionately refer to this question as the "truth serum" question because it has a way of getting customers to tell you how they really feel.

WHAT TO LISTEN FOR. Listen for replies like "Well, before I could recommend it, I'd have to see how..." The things customers want to see before they would recommend your concept are the factors you're interested in.

The value of this insight is that the customer is effectively telling you how they plan to "kick the tires" of your solution. If you were to release your concept today, these are the factors that customers would check to ensure your concept lives up to its promise.

HOW BELIEVABLE IS THIS CONCEPT AS A SOLUTION?

1	2	3	4	5

Not very
believable

Very
believable

WHY TO ASK THIS. The "believability" question will help you determine if your concept would be met with skepticism if it were released as a solution. At this point, you're showing the customer an early, conceptual idea. You haven't shown them any specific workflows or gone into depth about the specific implementation details.

WHAT TO LISTEN FOR. The customer might say, "I see what you're trying to do, but I don't think it can be done." They may have opinions about where your concept might fail in the market. This is the type of sentiment you're getting at with the believability score.

However, if the customer thinks your concept is believable and useful, it's a good indication that you'll be met by a market that's ready to adopt your solution.

HOW DIFFERENT IS THIS CONCEPT FROM OTHER SOLUTIONS CURRENTLY AVAILABLE?

1	2	3	4	5

Not at all
different

Very
different

WHY TO ASK THIS. Ideally, as you evolve your concept, you'll be keeping an eye on competitive solutions. The "uniqueness" question helps you identify if the customer finds your concept new and different from what the competition offers.

WHAT TO LISTEN FOR. This is also an opportunity for customers to offer any solutions you may be unaware of. Many customers find ways to solve their problems using their own tools or workarounds. Listen for customers who are happy with their own solutions. It may be an indication that, while your concept may be offering something your competitors don't, your customers are happily solving the problem on their own. In short, just because your concept is uniquely solving a problem, you shouldn't assume your customers need it.

Things to Consider While Creating a Concept Value Test

While the CVT will provide you a great, measured approach to getting feedback from your customers, there are some other things you should consider.

Have an Opinion

The most important aspect of the Concept Value Test is that it challenges you to have a clear, articulated opinion about how you plan to solve the problem. You might be asking, "Why don't I just show customers all of our concepts and have them tell me which one they like best?" This is an ineffective approach because you've moved the onus of solving the problem to the customer. It's not the customer's job to find the right solution—it's yours!

Therefore, encourage your team to have an opinion about the concept you're considering. If you genuinely welcome the customer's honest feedback, your customers will be willing to tell you if your opinion is lacking the right perspective.

You can certainly run multiple CVTs in parallel, but you should refrain from showing a single customer multiple CVTs that use different approaches to solve the same problem. First, it's cognitively overwhelming to evaluate multiple options, and second, customers can be biased to favor a concept, based on the order in which the concept was received.

To keep things simple, work together to come up with a single concept, test it with customers, and refine that concept based on customer feedback. You'll always have your alternatives in your back pocket, should you need them for future iterations.

Recognize That Concept Value Tests Are *Not* Usability Tests

One of the most valuable things about Concept Value Testing is the fact that it requires very little effort to put one together. We've successfully run CVTs without a single image, wireframe, or workflow. CVTs are *not* usability tests. In other words, we're not testing specific workflows, UI elements, or interactions. That sort of refinement will happen at the Feature stage.

Sharpen the Language Surrounding Your Concept

An extremely valuable byproduct of going through the CVT process is that teams learn how to effectively communicate their MVP. After talking with customers, ranking benefits and limitations, and examining rating scales, the team begins to understand what's important about the concept and what isn't. Throughout the process, your team will revise the words you use to describe the benefits and limitations of your concept. These words will be useful in the Feature stage, where you must clearly state what it is you're building (and what you're not building).

PartyTime Apps Revisited

The PartyTime Apps team was excited to start working on the details of their Potluck Planner Pack idea and begin showing it to customers. They began a series of customer calls, using a videoconferencing solution with screen-sharing capabilities.

They decided to start off by talking with customers that were already using their PartyOrganizr app. When the customer joined the video call, the team would share a slide presentation that walked them through the scenario, value proposition, benefits, and limitations of the concept.

To set the stage for customers, they come up with a simple scenario:

> Your boss has asked you to organize an annual office potluck party. You're responsible for creating the invitation and maintaining the attendee list for all 25 people on your team.

Customers really identified with this scenario and often shared examples of frustrations they had while planning potlucks. This gave the team even more validation that they'd found a problem worth solving. Next, the team revealed the unique value proposition for their concept:

> The Potluck Planner Pack is an add-on for PartyOrganizr that provides features for organizing and attending potluck parties.

Susan had sketched some low-fidelity storyboards that walked customers through a few high-level experiences (sending an invitation, adding dishes to the attendee list, etc.). The team showed the storyboards to customers and it helped them understand the basics of the concept.

Initial reactions to the value proposition and storyboards were positive, but customers had many follow-up questions. The team captured these questions and were delighted that many customers were asking for specifics that were addressed on the upcoming benefits slide. This was validation that the team had included the right features. Customers were really engaged as they tried to "fill in the gaps," and some even offered new ideas the team hadn't considered.

Next, the team revealed each benefit of the concept. They had a hard time settling on the features that the Potluck Planner Pack should include, but thanks to the Impact/Effort Matrix, they prioritized the benefits they believed had the greatest impact on planning a successful potluck.

The Potluck Planner Pack would:

- Allow party organizers to create a potluck event using a "potluck template." The template includes all the necessary components that make a successful potluck (date, location, dish categories, etc.).

- Allow guests to select a dish from the list of categories provided by the organizer.

- Send notifications to the organizer and attendees when a guest selects their dish.

- Provide a "recipe box." Customers can select dishes from their recipe box to bring to the party.

- Customers can search for new recipes ideas, right from the app, and add them to their recipe box.

The team was surprised to see a lackluster response to the recipe box idea. Jerry and his engineers were convinced this would be a killer feature and had already began building a prototype, but once they saw that customers were ranking it at the bottom of the list, they immediately abandoned the idea.

They also learned that managing the list of food everyone was bringing to the party was the "must have" feature. They were confident that, if they didn't land this functionality, the concept wouldn't be valuable for customers.

The team also showed customers a set of limitations. These were things the team thought might be important, but were too costly to implement in the first version. They wanted to know if any of these limitations would prevent customers from using the Potluck Planner Pack.

The Potluck Planner Pack would have the following limitations:

- Guests can't include a list of ingredients for the dish they plan to bring.
- Guests can't add their own dish categories (desert, snacks, side dishes, etc.).
- Guests can't indicate they're offering a dish but not attending the party.
- Guests can't indicate they're sharing a dish with another guest (e.g., two people are making a single casserole).
- This feature pack is an add-on. These features can be purchased separately in the app store.

The team was concerned that not having the ability to see the ingredients of each dish was going to be a dealbreaker for many of the customers. They had heard this problem expressed multiple times in their earlier interviews, but now customers didn't seem all that concerned about it.

Even customers who had food allergies felt that having to input recipe ingredients for the dish you planned to bring was too time-consuming. Many felt that, if they needed to, they could simply ask the person who made the dish if there were any ingredients they should be aware of.

This was a huge relief to the design team, because they were struggling with ideas on how customers could easily enter ingredients into the mobile app. Now that it didn't seem to be that big of a problem, they decided to focus their attention on getting other features right.

Customers seemed very concerned about the fact that the Potluck Planner Pack was being sold separately, but the concern was not what the team had expected. The team thought that customers would be really upset that they would have to pay for additional functionality, but this was not the case.

Customers were happy to purchase the add-on, but they were concerned that party guests would have to purchase the add-on as well for the functionality to work for everyone. If that were the case, customers didn't think they could convince everyone attending the potluck to purchase the add-on.

The team hadn't considered this limitation before. They decided that they would recommend that the add-on be marketed to party organizers.

In other words, if the potluck organizer purchased the add-on, they could create a potluck party that would be available to anyone who was using PartyOrganizr. They knew that it might cut down on the number of people purchasing the add-on, but the team believed it would ensure that the add-on would gain traction with customers.

The team was extremely happy with their rating scores. Not only did they have a lot of positive comments from customers, but the concept rated high in terms of solving a problem, willingness to try, and uniqueness when compared to other solutions. When customers were asked if they would be willing to recommend the concept to their friends, they said, "Absolutely!"

It appeared the team had landed on a great concept that customers were really excited to use. In fact, many customers asked, "When are you going to make this available? I need this today!"

In five weeks, half the time they were given, the team had a promising concept that was gaining traction. It was time to present their idea to leadership.

Susan and the team created a presentation that walked stakeholders through their process. They showed how they had pivoted from professional party planners and decided to "double down" on the customers they were already serving.

This was a surprise to many people in the room because the conventional thinking was that it was time to take PartyOrganizr to professional customers. Leadership was happy that the team had investigated that angle and finally put the idea to rest.

Throughout the project, the team continually refined their language and understanding of the problem space. They could passionately talk about the problem of planning potlucks, and they had tons of direct customer quotes to support their thinking.

It took little time to convince the room that it was a problem that PartyTime Apps was uniquely positioned to solve.

Finally, the team presented their concept for the Potluck Planner Pack add-on. They walked the group through the benefits and limitations, and offered a clear vision of what it would do (and not do). Finally, the team shared the feedback they had collected using CVTs and showed the high ratings the concept received from customers.

The CEO loved the add-on idea and was excited that customers seemed to support it. She quickly began offering ideas for other add-ons that could be investigated, using CVTs.

The team had hit a home run and got unanimous support to begin building the Potluck Planner Pack.

The team felt great knowing that they had landed on the right thing for their customers and the company. Now they just needed to figure out how to build it the right way.

Key Points

- How you understand, articulate, and frame the problems you're trying to solve directly impacts the eventual outcomes or solutions you provide.

- The best ideas come from teams who are willing to be "continuous and collaborative." They encourage everyone to contribute ideas and are willing to build off the ideas of others.

- Framing a problem by asking yourself, "How might we?" is a powerful way to unlock your team's creative potential.

- Consider using an Impact/Effort Matrix to prioritize your ideas. This will assess each idea by its direct impact on customers versus the cost to the team to develop it.

- A Concept hypothesis allows you to state your assumptions regarding your concept, such as whom it's for, what problem it solves, and how you plan to measure its success.

- A Concept Value Test (CVT) is a low-cost way to test early ideas with customers and get their feedback. It establishes whether your idea solves the customer's problem in a way that they believe is valuable.

- While working with a CVT, it's important for the team to have an opinion. Avoid showing customers multiple concepts that solve the same problem and having the customer choose which is the right solution. It's better to put a single concept for each problem in front of the customer and have them evaluate the value of the concept against the problem it's trying to solve.

- A CVT consists of a unique value proposition that explains the concept, a set of benefits and limitations, and a series of questions that allow the customer to rate the concept.

- During the CVT you'll have customers rank the benefits of the concept in order of "most impactful" to "least impactful." This helps you establish the MVP, or the core set of features that the concept must have to remain valuable to the customer.

- You'll also have the customer rank the limitations of the concept from "most impactful" to "least impactful." This helps the team avoid solving problems that are unimportant to the concept's value, and prevents them from ignoring dealbreaker issues that will prevent customers from using it.

- The CVT will give you qualitative and quantitative feedback for your concept. With this data, you'll be better equipped to explain exactly what the concept needs to be a valuable solution.

Endnotes

1 [99pi]
2 [rose]
3 [rose]
4 [daniels]
5 [kelly]
6 [basadur]
7 [basadur-innovation] p. 99
8 [gray]
9 [sony]
10 [howe]
11 [video]
12 [wielage]
13 [maurya]

[8]

The Feature

It was nearing the year 2000 and while everyone seemed to be worried about whether the world's computers would be obliterated by the Y2K bug, Heinz, an American food processing company, was focused on an entirely different problem.

People weren't buying ketchup.

To be clear, it wasn't that people had completely stopped buying the tomato-based product, it was that they were starting to eat healthier and that meant eating fewer hamburgers, fries, and hot dogs, which in turn meant they had little need for ketchup.

Heinz started the year with sales of ketchup hitting a plateau. It was, by far, their most successful product and they needed to act quickly to make sure that it stayed in homes for years to come.

They considered many different ideas to refresh the public's image of ketchup. One idea was to introduce a new line of ketchups, called EZ Squirt, that came in bold colors. The first color was green and was sold during the release of the movie *Shrek*. The company hoped that kids would eat the ketchup during the movie and develop a newfound love for the product.[1]

Parents and kids had fun with the new ketchup as a novelty, but it didn't really have lasting appeal. Heinz tried releasing new colors like blue and purple and even tried a "mystery color," where customers didn't know what color they were going to get. All the radically colored ketchups were met with lackluster sales.

Heinz also turned to more functional ideas. They explored what was preventing customers from using ketchup and discovered a common problem: their customers didn't like pouring it out of the bottle.

Ketchup, as a thick, slow-pouring condiment, "plops" onto your food. In fact, Heinz ketchup is so slow to pour that the company had begun to celebrate it. In a 1987 commercial, television star Matt LeBlanc stands atop a building and strategically places a ketchup bottle on the edge of the roof. The ketchup begins to pour, and LeBlanc runs down several flights of stairs to a hot dog vendor on the street. He casually buys a hot dog and, at the very last minute, places it behind his back to catch the perfect pour of ketchup, falling neatly from the roof. A voice confidently announces, "Heinz. The best things come to those who wait."[2]

The ad was popular during the 80s and early 90s, but by 2000, people weren't willing to wait for anything, even ketchup.

The company tried squeeze bottles to improve speed, but the ketchup would stick inside the bottle, plop out unevenly, and make embarrassing sounds the company politely referred to as "bottle flatulence."

It seemed like they were out of ideas.

Then Heinz discovered a man named Paul Brown. He was the owner of a small precision-molding shop in Midland, Michigan.[3] Paul had a crazy dream. He wanted to build the perfect nozzle, which would allow products like shampoo, lotion, and, yes, even ketchup, to be poured evenly from a plastic bottle.

What made Brown's idea so unique was that the nozzle sat at the *bottom* of the bottle. Effectively, the bottle sat upside-down.

Heinz knew it was the perfect solution to their problem.

Through iteration, they created a dispensing nozzle that opened easily when the bottle was squeezed and closed quickly when the pressure stopped, resulting in a seamless and even pour. The nozzle and bottle were wide enough for the bottle to stand upside-down and leave ketchup at the nozzle, ready to pour. They even created a new bottle shape that made it easy to store in the side door of customers' refrigerators (Figure 8-1).

When Heinz began testing the new bottle design, customers loved it. It was released in 2002 and the upside-down bottle quickly became a hit, winning Heinz numerous product awards and driving ketchup sales up nearly 25 percent.[4]

FIGURE 8-1
Heinz upside-down
ketchup bottle
(courtesy of Mike
Mozart via Flickr)

This is not a story of a man who had an ingenious, upside-down idea. It's a story of a company that knew that details mattered. They were willing to consider the entire experience of eating ketchup and refine a feature that had gone unnoticed.

As product creators, we must pursue our product's vision with the same level of care and craftsmanship.

The Feature stage of the HPF is designed for tracking the implementation and design of the features that make up your concept.

Throughout this book, we've talked about how we must move from understanding the customer to understanding their problems, and testing our early conceptual ideas to determine their validity. The Customer, Problem, and Concept stages come together to ensure that we are building the right thing for our customers. The Feature stage ensures that we are building it the right way (Figure 8-2).

During the Feature stage, we'll begin creating workflows, higher-fidelity mockups, and prototypes to ensure that customers will be successful when using our feature. We'll follow Lean principles and the Customer-Driven Cadence—formulating hypotheses, running Lean usability experiments, and making sense of the data to inform our next steps with the design.

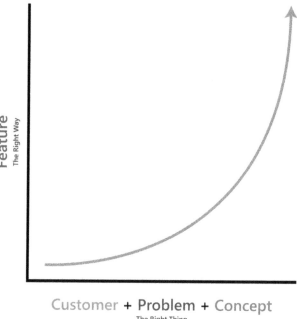

FIGURE 8-2
Building the right thing
versus building it the
right way

Feature
The Right Way

Customer + Problem + Concept
The Right Thing

Formulating a Feature Hypothesis

As in the previous stages of development, before you begin to test your features with customers, your team should understand what you're testing and what success will look like.

Like the Concept stage, the Feature hypothesis includes measurable criteria that will allow you to compare iterations and identify the factors that made one iteration more successful than another.

> We believe that [type of customers] will be successful solving [problem] using [feature] while doing [job-to-be-done].

> We will know they were successful when we see [criteria].

At this point, we have many of the parameters coming from previous stages. However, there are some new parameters:

[feature]

> The [feature] parameter is slightly different than the [concept] parameter introduced in the Concept stage. Here, we break down the concept into specific features and interactions.

As in the Concept stage, we will use measurable criteria to define what a successful test looks like. The goal is to have criteria that allow the team to remain objective.

Dr. Arnie Lund, Senior Research Manager at Amazon, measures usability with *a USE questionnaire*, which stands for Usefulness, Satisfaction, and Ease of use.[5]

These dimensions help us determine whether a feature was successful by asking ourselves:

- Were customers able to complete the task?

- Did they encounter any unexpected errors? How did they handle it?

- Throughout the task, did they understand what they were doing and why they were doing it?

- Were they efficient and accurate, or did they labor and become confused?

- Did they appear confident and satisfied?

- Did they need additional help and were they able to find it quickly?

Additionally, you can add questions to your Discussion Guide to ask about the customer's experience while using your prototype.

Talking with Customers About Your Features

When talking with customers about your feature, you want to create an experience where they can explore it themselves, not give them a demonstration of your product. It's important that customers tell you what *they* think your feature does; they shouldn't be listening to you explain it to them.

In fact, if your feature requires a lot of up-front explanation for customers to understand how it works, that might be a strong indication that you have usability problems. If customers are having a hard time navigating your usability study, you might consider:

Higher-fidelity compositions

Your screen compositions might be too vague, making it difficult for customers to determine what your feature does.

Smaller scenarios

Your feature may be too wide sweeping. It may be best to break up the experiences into smaller scenarios that customers can wrap their heads around.

The right customer

It's possible that you need to revisit the Customer stage and ensure you're targeting the right customer. Perhaps the customers you're talking to don't have the knowledge and experience to navigate the scenarios you're testing. Perhaps the customer you're targeting doesn't exist.

The right problem

You may have to return to the Problem stage to determine whether you're solving the right problem. If you're finding that customers are having difficulty understanding the problem you're trying to solve, there's a high probability that they simply don't have that problem.

When you're talking with customers during the Feature stage, the same rules apply as when you're talking to customers in the Customer, Problem, and Concept stages. You'll have to resist the urge to take control or tell the customer what to do.

In the real world, when your feature is released, your customers won't have the benefit of having you sit by them, telling them how to use it.

It's okay to let them struggle. Give them time to figure it out and encourage them to talk aloud, explaining what they're looking at and how they plan to interact with it. If you rush in to help, you'll miss key opportunities to learn how your customer will process and navigate your feature.

Formulating a Discussion Guide (with Tasks)

To get meaningful results, you need to ensure you're walking customers through the right tasks.

Once you've identified your tasks, capture them in your Discussion Guide, along with any other interview questions, so you can keep your experiment consistent between customers.

Additionally, have some questions prepared in the beginning to help you set context before you ask the customer to complete a task. You'll also include questions at the end to evaluate their overall satisfaction with the experience. Consider adding the rating scale questions you asked during the Concept stage to assess whether the feature is still solving a problem or is valuable for the customer.

It's important to note that, while you're testing the usability of your feature, it's still an opportunity to get feedback from your customer about their motivations, the problem you're trying to solve, and whether your feature is valuable to them.

In the book *Observing the User Experience: A Practitioner's Guide to User Research*, authors Elizabeth Goodman, Mike Kuniavsky, and Andrea Moed write that a good task should be:[6]

Reasonable

Don't test outliers or situations that rarely occur. You may be tempted to put your feature "through the ringer," but you don't want to optimize your design for extreme cases. Plus, it'll frustrate your customer if you're giving them a task that is too hard to complete.

Achievable

You should know what exact steps are needed to complete the task. If you've written down your Feature hypotheses, you should be anticipating what the customer will encounter as they navigate the task.

Specific

The task should be specific and have an understood outcome. You shouldn't ask, "How would you search for a service provider on our website?" Instead, you should say, "I'd like you to find a carpet cleaning service, located five miles from your location."

Sequential

Create a usability study that has customers progressing through a realistic sequence of events. Avoid having them bounce around from experience to experience. It may create unnecessary confusion and affect the results of your study.

PartyTime Apps Revisited

Susan and Mary began working with the design and engineering team to discuss feasibility and implementation of the Potluck Party Planner add-on.

With leadership's support, the project was starting to get a lot of attention. Engineering wanted to start work on rebuilding the underlying platform to support the add-on, and Design thought it would be the perfect time to unveil a redesign of PartyOrganizr they had been working on.

Mary was concerned that the project's scope was starting to creep and the team was losing sight of the original deliverable.

Thankfully, during the Concept stage, the team learned that one of the top benefits of their concept was the ability for party organizers and guests to add and update the dish they planned to bring to the party.

Mary suggested that, for now, the team should focus on the dish management scenario. If they're able to create a great experience around managing the potluck dishes, it will help inform all the remaining interactions of the add-on package. The team agreed and put their other projects on hold.

The design team reviewed the notes they had collected in their evidence file. Because the designers had spent time with real customers, they deeply understood them and had a better idea of the type of experiences that would delight them. In the past, the design team would've been asked to create a fictitious persona of the "ideal customer."

That would've led to countless hours of arguing amongst the designers about who understood the customer more. Not only were these arguments time-consuming and costly, they would also reduce the team's morale.

Now, they had recordings and notes of real people talking about the frustrations of organizing a potluck. They didn't need to create fake personas; they had actual customers they could reference!

The designers created some simple wireframes of the interface, showcasing adding, updating, and removing dishes from the Potluck Planner screen.

While the initial design was far from perfect, the team decided to test the basic interactions with customers as soon as possible, to ensure that the overall layout was something customers would understand and be successful with.

Throughout the process of navigating the HPF, the entire team had been talking with customers, and Mary had been keeping track of contact information for all the customers they spoke to.

PartyTime Apps now had a strong cohort of customers that they could talk to. These were customers who had said they were frustrated about organizing potlucks and were excited to be given a chance to help build the new feature. These customers felt like they were in an exclusive club. Not only did they feel like valued customers, they felt like they were partners on the project!

Before the first round of usability studies was conducted, the team created a set of Feature hypotheses. They focused on what outcomes they hoped to achieve with the new workflow and established criteria that could be objectively measured to determine whether the design was successful. They agreed that the dish management experience would be successful if customers could complete the core tasks. They made sure to include those tasks in the criteria of their Feature hypotheses:

> We believe that potluck attendees will be successful using the dish management screen when organizing a potluck.

> We will know they were successful when we see they can successfully create a potluck event.

The team identified other criteria that could be used to determine the design's success.

> We will know customers are successful when we see that they can:

- Understand who is coming to the party

- Understand what dish each guest is bringing

- Understand when another guest updates their dish

- Update the dish they plan to bring

- Remove the dish they are planning to bring

- Add a completely new dish to the list and assign themselves to it

- Decline the invitation and remove themselves from the party

Armed with these hypotheses, the team was ready to create a Discussion Guide that would walk customers through a sequential set of tasks, highlighting each experience they had formulated a hypothesis about. The Guide also included questions in the beginning to set context, and at the end to evaluate the entire experience.

Using the Discussion Guide, the design team could string together a series of mockups that simulated the experience. They organized them all into a deck, using a prototyping software.

Using the hypotheses, Discussion Guide, and prototype, Susan could walk customers through an organized usability study.

1. "I would like you to begin by creating a potluck and inviting Bob, Mary, and Joe to the party."

2. "We now want you to update the dish you're bringing. We'd like you to change it from tacos to pizza."

3. "Imagine you wanted to add dessert as an option for someone to bring to the party. Show me how you would do that."

4. "Tell me what you're seeing on the screen here."

5. "What do you think this notification is telling you?"

6. "You seem confused. Can you tell me what you're struggling with?"

Susan offered specific, but minimal, instruction. She was careful not to explain or demonstrate the dish management feature. If a customer was confused, Susan would ask questions and get the customer to think out loud. The team was listening in on the call and taking notes. Hearing the customers try to reason their way through the experience was incredibly insightful.

Finally, Susan asked the customer to rate their satisfaction with the overall experience, on a scale from 1 to 5. Susan asked the customer follow-up questions to understand the reasons for the score.

After the call was completed, the team would get together and discuss what they had learned from the study.

After a handful of calls, the team was ready to make refinements to the design. They noticed, during most of the calls, customers seemed confused that there were two different tabs, one for guests and one for dishes. Many of the customers didn't understand why you would have to switch to a different view to see the dishes attendees planned to bring. The designers made a small tweak to the design, placing the dish under the attendee's name. This way the customer could see the attendee and dish on the same screen.

The design team made many other changes and returned the following week to run the new designs through the same scenarios. After a few rounds, the team started to increase the fidelity, introducing brand colors and new interaction patterns.

In short order, the team was beginning to land the dish management screen with customers. This established many of the key design patterns that could be used for the entire experience.

Throughout the entire progression of the HPF, the team kept the customer's voice at the center of their decision-making. They solved the right problems in a way that customers found valuable and useful.

When the Potluck Planner Pack was finally released to the store, many of PartyTime Apps customers bought the add-on. By the end of the week, potlucks were the #1 party type being created in PartyOrganizr. Customer ratings for the app were up and customers were already requesting new add-ons. Revenue had nearly doubled and it was clear to everyone that, with the right add-ons, the company could triple their revenue by the end of the next fiscal year.

Susan and the team were proud of what they had accomplished in such short order. With the help of the HPF and the Customer-Driven Cadence, they were able to iterate quickly but stay focused and, above all, put the customer's voice at the center of their decision-making.

The best part of the customer-driven strategy was the positive relationship and continual feedback loop the team had created with its customers.

The team was already busy working on a concept for the next add-on, and Mary was scheduling for the next round of CVTs.

The entire company had become completely customer-driven.

Key Points

- The best product teams continually look for new opportunities to shape their products. If it solves a problem for customers, even small improvements can have big rewards.

- The Concept stage helps you design the right thing, whereas the Feature stage helps you design it the right way.

- Formulating Feature hypotheses is the best way to track your feature's iterations.

- When showing your feature to customers, you should allow the customer to tell *you* what they're seeing and how they would interact with it. Give them time to make sense out of what you're showing them; don't turn your usability study into a product demonstration.

- To have a useful usability study, it's important that you create the right tasks. Choose tasks that are reasonable and solvable. Be sure your tasks aren't so long that it causes the customer to feel overwhelmed or tired.

Endnotes

1 [glass]
2 [heinz-commercial]
3 [greve]
4 [mozart]
5 [lund]
6 [goodman] pp. 283–284

[9]

Using the Playbooks

We've walked you through each stage of the Hypothesis Progression Framework and followed the pattern of the Customer-Driven Cadence. If you haven't already, make sure to read the "PartyTime Apps Revisited" sections in this book. These sidebars are intended to be illustrative stories to help you understand how all the parts of our process come together.

If you're ready to start implementing the practices outlined in this book, we encourage you to start using the individual playbooks after this chapter. They've been designed for you to pick up and get started quickly. We imagine that you'll return to them often, until you get the swing of things.

Experiment Types

As we've discussed, there are many experiments that you can conduct to validate or invalidate your hypotheses. Each of the playbooks focuses on one experiment type (see Table 9-1). This was done out of necessity because we wanted to give you a single, end-to-end path through our methodology.

TABLE 9-1. The experiment type represented in each playbook

PLAYBOOK	EXPERIMENT TYPE
Customer	Customer visit
Problem	Interview
Concept	Concept Value Test
Feature	Usability study

Just because we use a particular experiment in one of the playbooks doesn't mean it's the *only* experiment you should run. For example, in the Customer playbook, we talk about conducting a customer visit; that doesn't mean you can't conduct a survey or a series of focus groups during the Customer stage as well. We encourage you to mix your experiments depending on your project needs.

Materials

To be successful with our playbooks, it's a good idea to have access to the following materials:

- Dry-erase markers, pens, and pencils
- Small (3×3) Post-it notes
- Medium (4×6) Post-it notes
- Large (5×8) Post-it notes
- A whiteboard or plenty of wall space
- Plenty of blank white paper
- Storyboard template (*customerdrivenplaybook.com*)
- Camera (using your phone is okay)
- Documenting software (e.g., Microsoft OneNote, Microsoft Excel, Google Sheets, Google Docs)

Roles and Responsibilities

We encourage your team to work through these playbooks together. However, the activities we present are more successful when you have one or two facilitators leading and moderating the discussion.

Table 9-2 lists some responsibilities for the facilitator and the rest of the team.

TABLE 9-2. Responsibilities for the facilitator and other team members

FACILITATOR	TEAM
Guide the process.	Freely express ideas.
Focus discussion on the topic— without limiting free exploration.	Withhold criticism or judgment— refrain from saying "that's a bad idea" or "that won't work."
Foster open expression of ideas.	Build on each other's input and allow others to build on your ideas.
Capture and display ideas.	Allow ideas to trigger new or unexpected thoughts.
Ensure participants/team fulfill their roles equally.	Be attentive and willing to contribute.
Gather necessary material for the activity.	
Secure a space/conference room to conduct activity.	

Part II

The Playbooks

[10]

The Customer Playbook

Conducting Customer Visits to Learn More About Your Customers

> We believe [type of customers] are motivated to [motivation] when doing [job-to-be-done].

This playbook is organized into three sections that align with the Customer-Driven Cadence:

Formulating

- Capture your team's assumptions about the parameters of the Customer hypothesis [type of customers], [motivation], and [job-to-be-done].

- Turn those assumptions into testable hypotheses.

- Generate a Discussion Guide to be used during the customer visit.

Experimenting

- Organize and prepare for your customer visit.

- Conduct a customer visit.

- Debrief after the customer visit is complete.

Sensemaking

- Use a structured method to derive patterns and meaning out of the customer data your team has collected from the customer visit.

- Share your customer insights with your organization.

Formulating

Formulating Customer Assumptions

1. CAPTURE ASSUMPTIONS.

Before jumping into formulating your hypotheses, you'll want to capture your team's assumptions about the type of customers you're targeting, their motivations, and job-to-be-done.

1. For each of the assumption prompts listed below, write your response on a Post-it note. You may have more than one response per prompt—that's expected! Capture one response per note.

   Assumption prompts for [type of customers]:

   > We are targeting _____ [type of customers].

   > These [type of customers] work in teams/organizations that are _____.

   > These [type of customers] are skilled in _____.

   > These [type of customers] are at _____ stage of their career.

   > These [type of customers] have _____ job title.

   > These [type of customers] are building _____ types of products, applications, or services.

   > These [type of customers] are experiencing the following market pressures: _____.

   > These [type of customers] use the following tools, platforms, and technologies to achieve their goals: _____.

   Assumption prompts for [motivation]:

   > These customers are motivated by _____.

   > These customers are influenced by _____.

   Assumption prompts for [job-to-be-done]:

   > These customers are focused on doing [job-to-be-done].

   > We want to help customers achieve _____.

> When customers engage in [job-to-be-done], they're doing the following tasks: _____.
>
> When engaged in [job-to-be-done], these customers often enlist the help of _____.

2. Place each Post-it note on the wall or board. Don't overthink it. Fill up the wall with as many Post-it notes as possible (Figure 10-1).

3. Complete this part of the exercise individually. Later, you will have time to clarify what you've put on the wall. At this point, you don't want to influence the team with your own assumptions.

4. Add duplicate notes. If one of your assumptions is already on the wall, put yours up on the wall too. Duplication is a good thing! It means the team shares the same assumptions.

FIGURE 10-1
All the team's assumptions on Post-it notes, hanging on the wall

2. ORGANIZE ASSUMPTIONS.

1. Once your team has captured their assumptions on Post-it notes, you'll want to organize them.

2. One the wall or board, draw three columns.

3. Using medium Post-it notes, label the columns [type of customers], [job-to-be-done], and [motivation].

4. Take each assumption Post-it note and place it in one of the columns. If you used the assumption prompts you should find a 1:1 mapping of category to Post-it note (Figure 10-2).

FIGURE 10-2

The team hangs
the assumption
Post-it notes under
three columns:
[type of customers],
[job-to-be-done],
and [motivation]

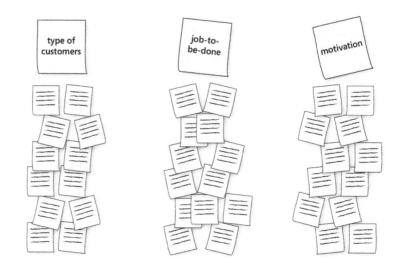

[NOTE]

To learn more about
why we create
a shoebox, see
Chapter 4.

3. DOCUMENT ASSUMPTIONS.

1. Take a picture of the wall to capture the categorized assumptions.

2. Tabulate all assumptions in a document, such as an Excel or OneNote file.

3. Create a shoebox to store the team's assets. Use a tool such as Microsoft OneNote, Evernote, Basecamp, Google Drive, or Dropbox to keep the assumptions you've captured.

Formulating Customer Hypotheses

1. FORMULATE HYPOTHESES.

To formulate a good Customer hypothesis, use the team's assumptions to populate the [parameters] in the following Customer hypotheses template. Write the Customer hypothesis on the wall or board large enough for the group to add Post-it notes to the [parameters].

> We believe [type of customers] are motivated to [motivation] when doing [job-to-be-done].

2. CAPTURE THE [TYPE OF CUSTOMERS].

1. Revisit the customer assumptions that were categorized into three columns: [type of customers], [job-to-be-done], and [motivation].

2. Select one customer from the [type of customers] column. Don't spend too much time thinking about which customer to start with; you'll get a chance to create hypotheses for all your target customers.

3. Place the type of customer Post-it note on the hypothesis template to fill in the blank parameter. If you have multiple types of customers, that's great! Capture each target customer in a separate hypothesis.

4. Be specific about the customer you're targeting. Consider the customer's skills, title, organization type, tools they use, and so on. If you have the customer's attributes captured on a Post-it note, add it to the hypothesis. If not, write the attributes on a Post-it note and add it to the hypothesis.

For example, your hypothesis may look like this:

> We believe [administrators] are motivated to [motivation] when doing [job-to-be-done].

You'll want to be more specific about the type of administrators you're targeting.

> We believe [office administrators working for a small business] are motivated to [motivation] when doing [job-to-be-done].

By including the specific attributes "office" and "small business," the team knows exactly which type of customer they're targeting.

3. CAPTURE THE [MOTIVATION].

1. Revisit the [motivation] column of assumptions.

2. What motivates this customer? Select one motivation Post-it note and place it on the hypothesis template to fill in the blank motivation parameter.

4. CAPTURE THE [JOB-TO-BE-DONE].

1. Revisit the [job-to-be-done] column of assumptions. You may find that the customer has multiple jobs related to their motivation. Capture each job in a separate hypothesis.

2. Place the [job-to-be-done] Post-it note on the hypothesis template to fill in the blank parameter.

5. DISCUSS.

As a team, review your hypotheses and consider:

- Does the team have a shared understanding of their target customers, motivations, and job-to-be-done?

- Can you identify any gaps in the team's knowledge related to the types of customers you're targeting?

- Are your hypotheses too vague? Do they include specific attributes such as work environment, skill, and/or job title?

6. REPEAT.

1. Continue to articulate all your assumptions into hypotheses. If you find that you need to write additional Post-it notes or need to duplicate an assumption you've already captured in another hypothesis, simply create a new Post-it note.

2. Write all your hypotheses on the board or wall.

3. Stand back and evaluate the number of hypotheses that the team has generated.

4. Revise hypotheses until the team comes to an agreement.

[NOTE]
To learn more about why we create evidence files, see Chapter 4.

7. RECORD.

1. Take a picture of the wall or board to capture all your hypotheses. This can serve as your backup if the wall gets erased.

2. Tabulate all your hypotheses in a document, such as an Excel or OneNote file. This document serves as your team's backlog.

3. Keep the backlog of hypotheses in the team's evidence file. Your evidence file captures only the meaningful bits of data that comprise your point of view, vision, or strategy for your product. It can help the team stay organized and up-to-date on the latest findings.

Formulating a Discussion Guide

Starting a conversation with customers isn't always easy. While it may be tempting to ask your customer lots of questions, be judicious and only ask questions that will help you test your Customer hypotheses.

The following Discussion Guide is a list of questions that align with your hypotheses. Edit the guide to include the parameters you defined in your Customer hypotheses. These questions will help you learn about the customer's work environment, jobs, and motivations. You should use these questions to get you started and revise or create new questions, if necessary.

1. FORMULATE QUESTIONS THAT VALIDATE [TYPES OF CUSTOMERS].

- What is your work environment like (e.g., size, physical surrounds, process maturity)?
- What are some of the market pressures your company faces?
- What things about your work environment would you characterize as being typical of other companies, and what things would you say are unique or exceptional?
- What is your job title and what are your primary responsibilities at your company?
- During your day, what type of tasks do you perform?
- Given your job role, what kind of skills, experiences, and personal characteristics do you need?
- What platforms, tools, and technologies do you commonly use?
- What other types of people do you work with?

2. FORMULATE QUESTIONS THAT VALIDATE [JOB-TO-BE-DONE].

- When doing [job-to-be-done] what are some of the specific jobs/tasks you perform?
- How often are you personally involved in [job-to-be-done]?
- Tell me who is involved in [job-to-be-done] at your company?
- Tell me about how you do [job-to-be-done] today.
- Is there anything specific that you typically do before or after you do [job-to-be-done]?
- Are there multiple starting points for [job-to-be-done]? If so, what are they?
- What products, services, or technologies do you or others at your company currently use when doing [job-to-be-done]?
- Tell me about the last time you did [job-to-be-done].

3. FORMULATE QUESTIONS THAT VALIDATE [MOTIVATION].

- What motivates you to do [job-to-be-done]?

- If you didn't do [job-to-be-done], what would be the consequences?

- When you do a good job at [job-to-be-done], what does it look like? How do you feel?

- When you start [job-to-be-done], what are you typically trying to achieve?

- What are the benefits of [job-to-be-done]? What do you or your company get out of it?

4. FORMULATE QUESTIONS THAT EXPAND YOUR CUSTOMER FEEDBACK LOOP.

- Is there anyone else that I should also be talking with? Is there anyone you know who is [type of customers]?

- May I contact you in the future if I have additional questions?

- In the future, if we had some early product ideas around [job-to-be-done], would that be something you'd be interested in seeing?

[NOTE]
For more information about creating a shoebox, see Chapter 4.

5. DOCUMENT YOUR DISCUSSION GUIDE.

Once you have decided on the questions you'll ask during your interview, collect them into a document and store it in your shoebox for the team to refer to when conducting their experiment.

Experimenting

Customer visits are the highest-fidelity and deepest customer learning you can experience. With customer visits, you can immerse yourself in the customer's world and get a sense of what motivates them, the jobs they perform, and the problems they face.

Preparing for a Customer Visit

1. FIND CUSTOMERS.

Gaining access to a customer's home or workplace can be challenging. Depending on their level of comfort and desire for privacy, you may find it difficult to get the proper clearance for you and your team to be onsite.

Plan to invest a lot of effort into finding potential customers to visit. Expect that your team will need to personally contact customers to develop a rapport before visiting with them.

Here are some things to consider when contacting customers for customer visits:

- Customers are more likely to invite you into their home or workplace if they trust you. An introduction from a friend or colleague can help cut through any hesitations.

- Reach out to personal connections that have established customer relationships. Start with consultants, sales, advisory councils, marketing, and so on.

- Once you get a potential customer visit contact, personally call them. Try to handle most of your initial contact face-to-face or over the phone. This will help foster a personal relationship prior to the customer visit.

- Have a primary point of contact that can help you with logistics, setting up, or any other travel information you may need.

2. SORT OUT THE LOGISTICS.

Before you visit the customer, make sure you have the details worked out. These details may seem trivial, but they will ensure you have a successful, well-planned visit. The more planning you do before the visit, the fewer surprises you'll encounter onsite.

Use the following checklist to ensure you've got it all covered:

- Have a contact name and number of the customer you're visiting.

- Share travel plans and contact information with the team.

- Make sure you have all equipment, and that it's in good working condition and charged.

- Create an agenda for the visit and have it approved by the customer.

- Determine the appropriate gratuity.

[NOTE]
For more information about the roles used in customer visits, see Chapter 3.

3. IDENTIFY ROLES.

Establish responsibilities for each team member before the customer visit. Here are some key roles you may want to establish:

Project lead/moderator

The project leader is the point of contact for everything internal and external across all the customer visits. This person will also serve as the moderator during the customer visit. He or she will be responsible for establishing and maintaining a partnership with the customer.

Offsite coordinator

A team member who is not attending the customer visit and can coordinate any last-minute incidents or logistics issues.

Note taker

Everyone except the project leader/moderator should consider themselves a note taker. Note takers are responsible for capturing every word that is communicated during the visit.

Videographer/photographer

The responsibilities of the videographer and photographer are to capture *everything*; you can edit later. Make sure you get permission to record or photograph before and during your visit. While onsite, the photographer should make it a habit to introduce themselves to anyone they encounter, before they begin to take pictures or record video.

4. HAVE A PLANNING MEETING.

It's a good idea to have a few planning meetings, prior to your customer visit, to organize the team and get everyone on the same page. It will also allow you to answer questions your team may have before visiting with the customer.

Important information to cover during training:

- The goals of the customer visit and the expected outcome
- The Discussion Guide
- Identifying roles
- The customer/team relationship
- Dress code
- Travel plans
- Schedule

5. GATHER YOUR MATERIALS.

You'll want to bring everything you need with you onsite, but you don't want your bags and equipment to get in the way or be a distraction. If you take care of the logistics and paperwork before the visit, you can pack just the essentials.

Checklist of equipment and materials you'll need for your visit:

- Video camera (we use GoPros—they're small, lightweight, and unobtrusive)
- Digital camera
- Laptop and notepads
- Pens/pencils
- Business cards
- Discussion Guide

Conducting a Customer Visit

There are four basic phases for conducting a customer visit. The structure of the visit can vary depending on the time and location of the visit. You'll want to modify the approach depending on the customer's workplace.

1. SET UP.

PROJECT LEAD/MODERATOR: Determine where you'll be observing the customer. This may be multiple locations, so be prepared to move. Have the Discussion Guide available. You'll refer to it during the customer visit to ensure you're capturing all the information you need to test your hypotheses.

NOTE TAKER: Create a shared location for your notes. Tools like OneNote and Evernote are helpful in syncing notes across multiple devices.

VIDEOGRAPHER/PHOTOGRAPHER: Set up equipment to ensure you have a good angle to capture the customer and their work environment. If possible, consider doing a test of your microphone to ensure you're able to hear the customer while recording.

2. MAKE THE INTRODUCTIONS.
PROJECT LEAD/MODERATOR:

1. Introduce yourself and the team. Explain your role in your organization.

2. Share your goals and expected outcomes.

3. Thank the participants for allowing you to partner with them while you observe their activities.

4. Explain the schedule and the structure of the visit. Make any adjustments as needed.

5. Encourage the customer to complete tasks as if they were not being observed.

6. Confirm that you can record and take pictures of them.

NOTE TAKER: Record the date, time, and the team members that are participating in the customer visit.

VIDEOGRAPHER/PHOTOGRAPHER: Begin recording once permission has been granted.

3. CONDUCT THE INTERVIEW.

PROJECT LEAD/MODERATOR: The first questions you ask the customer should be "icebreakers," simple questions to make the customer feel comfortable. Typically, asking the customer about their role at work, the activities they engage in, or the tools and technology they use are good warm-up questions. Refer to your Discussion Guide for the icebreakers.

At the beginning of the visit, it's important to set the tone and establish a partnership with the customer, rather than an interview/interviewee or guest/host relationship. To establish a partnership with the customer:

- Let the customer lead.

  - Strive to observe the natural course of events; don't "manufacture" them.

  - Document what you see, hear, and feel, but try not to react.

  - Ask open-ended, nonbiased, and neutral questions.

- Say "show me."

  - When possible, have the customer demonstrate rather than describe the situations they typically encounter.

  - Show interest in what the customer is showing you and ask clarifying questions to ensure you fully understand what you're observing. Customers will appreciate your desire to capture as much as of their situation as possible.

  - When you observe something that interests you, ask follow-up questions that help you understand the context and motivations of the behavior. If necessary, ask the customer to show you again, so that you can be sure to capture it.

- Learn, don't teach.

  - Customers may be nervous, because they see you as the "expert." Continually reassure them that you are there to learn about their unique situations. Position *them* as the expert.

  - Because they have "experts" on site, customers may try to get you to help them solve their issues with your product. As best you can, try to refrain from your visit turning into a support call. If you need to offer support services, you may suggest leaving an hour or two, in your agenda, to diagnose issues with the customer or log bugs.

- Don't immediately help the customer. Customer visits are where you get to directly observe customers' frustrations and workarounds.

- Help the customer only when you know they have hit a wall and can't move forward.

- Assume nothing.

- Check your assumptions with the user.

- If you need clarity, it's okay to stop the customer and ask for clarification.

NOTE TAKER: Try your best to capture everything the customer is saying. Do not paraphrase. Capture everything:

- Capture what you see, hear, and feel in the moment.

- Pay attention to the customer's body language.

- Do not interpret or summarize during the visit.

- Use the customer's words, not yours. If you can, get direct quotes.

- Create sketches, workflows, and keyframes to enhance what you're observing.

VIDEOGRAPHER/PHOTOGRAPHER: Ensure that the video recording has started. Take pictures of the customer and their environment, the tools that they use, and the people they interact with.

4. OBSERVE.

This is the part of the study where the team will learn the most. You'll be embedded in a rich environment where there are a lot of stimuli to attend to.

Everyone attending the customer visit should focus on activities the customer performs, the environment they're operating in, objects they use, and the customer's behaviors, preferences, and needs.

This slightly modified version of the AEIOU framework[1] will help you and the team interpret the data that you're observing and tag it in a meaningful way to interpret later:

Activities

The actions and process that the customer experiences while trying to accomplish a task/job. Things to consider while observing customer activities:

- Noteworthy tasks/activities
- Events or milestones
- The amount of concentration required
- Field of attention
- Quality of the feedback they are provided
- Balance between ability and challenge
- Control they have over the activity

Environment

The physical and technological environmental factors that shape their experience. Things to consider when observing the customer's environment:

- Shared spaces, offices, or cubicles
- Centralized teams or dispersed
- Closed or open platforms

Interpersonal interactions

The interactions the customer has with the team/group/community and how that effects their experience. Things to consider while observing customer interactions with a group:

- Goals and strategy
- Process or methodology
- Communication patterns
- Social structures
- Culture

Objects

The tools and artifacts the customer uses that impacts their experience. Things to consider when observing the customer use tools:

- ○ Competitor tools

- ○ Homegrown tools

- ○ Gaps in their tooling needs

Users/customers

The individual differences or attributes that affect how they behave, think, and feel:

- ○ Learning preference

- ○ Cognitive style

- ○ Experience/skill

- ○ History

5. WRAP UP.

PROJECT LEAD/MODERATOR:

- Throughout the day, you should be watching and listening for signals that validate or invalidate your hypotheses. As you bring the conversation to an end, revisit the Discussion Guide and determine if there are additional topics that you need to discuss or observe.

- Ask the note taker and videographer if they have any questions or need clarity on any topics.

- Thank the customer for their willingness to have your team onsite.

- Remind the customer that they can contact you if they would like to follow up or have any questions.

- If you didn't already provide gratuity, do so before you leave the site.

NOTE TAKER:

- Review your notes and determine if you need any more detail. When the Project Lead opens the conversation, ask the customer any questions that can help clarify what you captured.

- When the notes are complete, be sure to include them in the team's shoebox.

VIDEOGRAPHER/PHOTOGRAPHER:

- Stop the recording.

- If possible, keep the recording and any pictures in your shoebox or another shared location.

Debriefing After Customer Visits

It's crucial that you allow time after the visit to meet with the team and discuss your observations. Here some things to consider during the debriefing:

- Include all team members that participated in the customer visit.

- Discuss what they felt, saw, and heard.

- Review and verify observations.

- Review the notes and determine if they fully capture the conversation and events that transpired.

- Capture meaningful information (direct quotes, surprising findings, context tools, etc.).

- All the artifacts you collected during your visits are valuable. Keep everything in the shoebox for safekeeping and future reflection.

- Pull the most meaningful data, notes, pictures, direct customer quotes, or any other type of signal that validates or invalidates your hypotheses and place it in your team's evidence file.

Sensemaking

Once the team has completed a series of customer visits, it's time to interpret your interviews and observations. As a team, you'll want to work together to review all the interview notes and begin to extract meaning out of the data you've captured. Working together, while analyzing data, ensures that the team has a shared understanding about the conclusions that were made.

Schematizing the Data

1. PRINT OUT ALL YOUR INTERVIEW NOTES.

1. Return to your team's evidence file and print the customer visit notes. Make enough copies of each customer visit notes so each team member has a copy.

   Through the playbook, we've encouraged documenting the outcome of each activity and placing it in your team's evidence file. It should now contain the most meaningful bits of data that comprise your point of view, vision, or strategy for your product.

   If you find that your evidence file is light and doesn't contain the data to validate or invalidate your hypotheses, go back to the shoebox and cull and organize the data you've collected along your journey and capture it in your evidence file.

2. Write a unique number or ID on the upper-right corner of each set of interview notes. This ID will allow you to relate the data you find to the specific customer.

3. Hand each team member one printed copy of an interview, a marker, and a stack of Post-it notes.

2. CAPTURE ANYTHING MEANINGFUL.

1. Thoroughly read the customer's interview notes.

2. When you find something meaningful, jot it down on a Post-it note. Here are some things you should be looking for:

   ◦ Direct quotes

   ◦ The customer's environment

   ◦ Jobs they are performing

- Motivations
- Skills
- Tool use
- Expressed frustrations or limitations
- Delighters

Don't overthink it—write a sentence or two to capture your finding on a Post-it and then move on.

3. For each customer you've visited, capture their data on different colored Post-it notes. By color-coding them you'll be able to easily track and visualize each customer's meaningful data. You'll need this later when you tell the story about each customer the team visited.

3. TAG THE DATA.

Data tagging will allow your team to organize the data in an efficient way. Use Table 10-1 to get started. Feel free to modify it as necessary.

TABLE 10-1. Suggested tags for schematizing your data

TAG	TYPE OF FEEDBACK
Motivation	Comments that give you an indication of the customer's motivation
Frustration/problem	Statements or observations that indicate a problem, frustration, limitation, or constraint
Jobs-to-be-done	Actions or tasks that you observe customers are engaging in to achieve their goals
Attribute	Individual differences or characteristics that help define the customer
Interpersonal interaction	Communications or interactions you witnessed the customer having with another team member or client
Environment	Details that describe the context in which you observed the customer
Tool	Any tools that you witnessed your customer using to achieve their goals

Using these tags, determine the nature of the customer data point that you captured and write it in the upper-right corner of your Post-it note. For example, if the data point had something to do with the customer's frustration, it should be tagged with an "F." Additionally, write the customer ID from the interview on the upper-left corner of the Post-it note (see Figure 10-3). If necessary, modify or create new tags to fit the needs of your team.

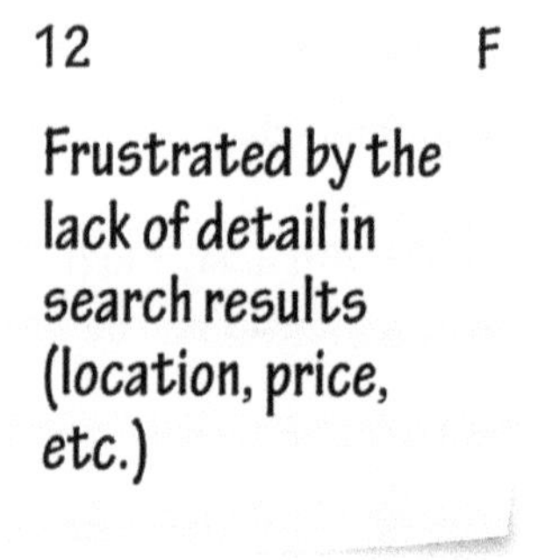

12   **F**

Frustrated by the lack of detail in search results (location, price, etc.)

FIGURE 10-3
A completed Post-it note for this exercise should be tagged with an interview ID (upper-left corner), a keyword tag (upper-right corner), and a brief description of the finding

Avoid the temptation of discussing the notes with the team. This gives each member enough time to focus on the interview notes, rather than discussing and comparing findings.

It also prevents the group from making premature conclusions, before all the customer visits have been reviewed. You'll get a chance to share your findings in the next step.

4. DISCUSS THE DATA.

Once the Post-it notes have been gathered on the wall, give your team a chance to discuss each customer's customer visit. Here are suggestions that can enrich the conversation:

- Give the team time to talk about each customer you've visited. Let them walk through what they learned and what stood out to them.

- Other team members should ask questions to clarify what was learned. If the original interviewer or note taker is in the room, allow them to add further details that might not have been picked up in the notes.

- Discuss if there is more to learn from the customer. If so, there may be an opportunity for the interviewer to call the customer back or email some follow-up questions.

- Repeat until you have discussed all the customers your team visited.

5. ORGANIZE AND GROUP THE DATA.

Now that you've captured all the customers you've visited, you should start to notice some general themes or duplication. Organize the Post-it notes into groups or similarities (see Figure 10-4). Here are some suggestions to help make this a productive process:

- It's important to be flexible here. If someone on the team objects to combining a couple of items, don't force it. Just move on to more obvious pairings.

- Revise groups and rearrange notes until the team comes to an agreement.

- Look for patterns or gaps in your groupings and continue the discussion:

  - Which areas seem to have the largest groups? Frustrations? Motivations? Are there tags that are underrepresented? If so, were you asking the right questions to drive out those details?

  - Which items have the most duplication? Why was the team hearing that response frequently?

  - Is the same data frustration or motivation expressed in different words? What's the best way to summarize that learning?

  - Are there customer types that are underrepresented? Why are they not represented on the wall?

  - Are there common workarounds or tools used by customers?

FIGURE 10-4
Flattening, grouping, and organizing interview data by keyword; here the team added their own tags as well

[NOTE]

For more information
on the evidence file,
see Chapter 4.

Updating the Evidence File

Now that your team has spent time schematizing the data, update your evidence file. It should contain the most meaningful bits of data that comprise the team's point of view, vision, and product strategy, including:

- A backlog of validated and invalidated hypotheses

- Attributes of the types of customers that are represented in your data

- Customer quotes that exemplify a motivation, frustration, desire, or the like

- Data points from external sources (market research, competitive analysis, etc.) that support your conclusions

Creating and Sharing Your Stories

After you've had time to interpret the data and discuss the learnings, you'll want to share what you've learned about your customers. You can do that by telling a compelling story and determining a way to share it.

TELL INDIVIDUAL CUSTOMER STORIES

Tell the story of each customer you visited. To bring their stories to life and build empathy, you'll want to include what the customer said, what they did, and how they felt.

Here's a list of materials that can be used to tell a great story:

Pictures

A picture of the customer, their work environment, and anything that exemplifies the customer.

Great quotes

Nothing is better than hearing the customer's direct feedback and voice.

Video

Create short clips that capture meaningful moments.

Here are some topics you can include in your stories:

- The sequence of activities and behaviors that shaped the customer's experience

- Environmental and technical factors that affected their experiences

- Coordination or interactions with others in their team/group/community

- The tools and artifacts they used and how it shaped their experience

- Individual differences—attributes that make each customer unique—and how they affect their job, tasks, or interactions with others

CREATE A SYNOPSIS OF CUSTOMER STORIES

In addition to the stories about the individual customers you visited, you'll want to communicate the overarching customer learnings. Were there common tensions, frustrations, or triggers that emerged across the visits? You'll want to share those insights in a way that others can easily consume and understand.

Consider communicating the meaning of your data in the following ways:

- Find a parallel or analogy that helps express the motivations of your customers. Using an example that is outside your domain, but understood by everyone, can be a helpful way to take an abstract learning and make it more accessible to a broader audience.

- Draw diagrams or models that illustrate conflicting tensions (e.g., customers want high quality but also want to save money). Two-by-two tension models can help articulate these conflicts.

- Create a timeline or journey map that shows the progression of a customer's journey while performing a job. Take note of key milestones or opportunities for engagement.

As customer advocates, share the information you have learned about your customers with your organization using the channels you've established as a team (standups, email alias, presentations, Slack channels, or newsletters).

Leverage existing channels first, but keep in mind that customer empathy and emotion can get lost in a sea of email inboxes. Consider additional ways to share the rich stories about your customers.

We've found that having photographs of the customer, their work environments, and printouts of direct quotes can be powerful imagery that helps bring customers to life. We've been successful sharing our stories by creating a physical location to visually display these types of customer materials. By displaying them in a location that gets moderate to heavy foot traffic, you'll get your organization's attention and interest.

Endnote

1 [AEIOU]

[11]

The Problem Playbook

Interviewing Customers About Their Problems and Frustrations

> We believe [type of customers] are frustrated by [job-to-be-done] because of [problem].

This playbook is organized into three sections that align with the Customer-Driven Cadence:

Formulating

- Capture your team's assumptions about the [problem] parameter of the Problem hypothesis by exploring customers' problems and frustrations.

- Turn those assumptions into testable hypotheses.

- Generate a Discussion Guide for conducting your interview.

Experimenting

- Prepare for customer interviews.

- Conduct customer interviews.

- Debrief after the interview is complete.

Sensemaking

- Use a structured method to derive patterns and meaning out of your customer interviews.

- Share your customer insights with your organization.

Formulating

Formulating Problem Assumptions

1. CAPTURE ASSUMPTIONS.

At each stage of the HPF, you'll want to capture your assumptions and turn them into testable hypotheses. In the Problem stage, if you don't validate that your customers are, in fact, having a problem and that it's painful enough for them to seek a resolution, you'll end up building solutions in search of a problem.

As a team, you'll want to capture your team's assumptions about the problems you believe your customers are experiencing.

1. For each of the assumption prompts listed below, write your response on a Post-it note. You may have more than one response per prompt—that's expected! Capture one response per note.

> These [type of customers] are lacking the _____ that they need to get their job done.

> This [problem] affects these [types of customers] in the following ways: _____.

> These [type of customers] are doing _____ to work around their problem.

> These [type of customers] experience pain when they are [job-to-be-done].

> This [problem] is small, but happens frequently.

> This [problem] occurs infrequently, but is critical.

> These [type of customers] have abandoned _____ because of _____.

> These [type of customers] are spending _____ amount of time doing _____.

> These [type of customers] are limited or constrained by _____.

> These [type of customers] want to do [job-to-be-done] today but can't, because [problem].

2. Place each Post-it note on the wall or board. Don't overthink it. Fill up the wall with as many Post-it notes as possible (Figure 11-1).

3. Complete this part of the exercise individually. Later, you will have time to clarify what you've put on the wall. At this point, you don't want to influence the team with your own assumptions.

4. Add duplicate notes. If one of your assumptions is already on the wall, put yours up on the wall too. Duplication is a good thing! It means the team shares the same assumptions.

FIGURE 11-1
All the team's assumptions on Post-it notes, hanging on the wall

2. ORGANIZE ASSUMPTIONS.

1. Once your team has captured their assumptions on Post-it notes, you'll want to organize them.

2. On the wall or board, draw three columns.

3. Using medium Post-it notes, label the columns [type of customers], [job-to-be-done], and [problem].

4. Take each assumption Post-it note and place it in one of the columns (see Figure 11-2).

5. If you find that your customers and job column are light, refer to your team's shoebox to locate the backlog of validated customer hypotheses. Capture the missing [parameters] on Post-it notes and place them on the wall or board.

FIGURE 11-2
The team hangs
the assumption
Post-it notes under
three columns labeled
[type of customers],
[job-to-be-done],
and [problem].

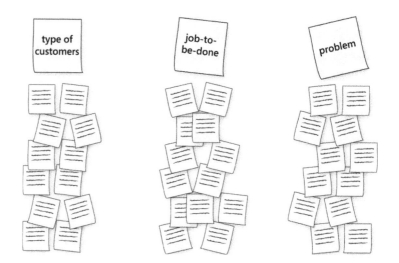

[NOTE]
To learn more about
why we create
a shoebox, see
Chapter 4.

3. DOCUMENT ASSUMPTIONS.

1. Take a picture of the wall to capture the notes, labels, and clusters.

2. Tabulate all assumptions in a document, such as an Excel or OneNote file.

3. Keep all documented assumptions in the team's shoebox.

Formulating Problem Hypotheses

1. FORMULATE HYPOTHESES.

To formulate a good Problem hypothesis, use the assumptions the team generated to populate the [parameters] in the following Problem hypotheses template. Write the Problem hypothesis on the wall or board large enough for the group to add Post-it notes to the [parameters].

> We believe [type of customers] are frustrated by [job-to-be-done] because of [problem].

2. CAPTURE THE [TYPE OF CUSTOMERS].

1. Revisit the customer assumptions that were categorized into the three columns [type of customers], [job-to-be-done], and [problem].

2. Select one customer from the [type of customers] column.

3. Place the type of customer Post-it note on the hypothesis template to fill in the blank parameter. If you have multiple types of customers, that's great! Capture each target customer in a separate hypothesis.

3. CAPTURE THE [JOB-TO-BE-DONE].

1. Revisit the [job-to-be-done] column of assumptions.

2. Place the [job-to-be-done] Post-it note on the hypothesis template to fill in the blank parameter.

4. CAPTURE THE [PROBLEM].

1. Revisit the [problems] column of assumptions.

2. Place the problem Post-it note on the hypothesis template to fill in the blank parameter.

3. Multiple types of customers may have the same problem. Capture them as separate hypotheses.

5. DISCUSS.

As a team, review your hypotheses and consider:

- Does the team have a shared understanding of their target customers and job-to-be-done?

- Are your hypotheses focusing on the customer's limitations instead of the team's limitations?

- Can you identify any gaps in the team's knowledge related to the problems customers are facing?

- Are your hypotheses segmenting types of customers correctly, or are they generalizing problems to all types of customers?

6. REPEAT.

1. Continue to articulate all your assumptions into hypotheses.

2. Write all your hypotheses on the board or wall.

3. Stand back and evaluate the number of hypotheses that the team has generated.

4. Revise hypotheses until the team comes to an agreement.

[NOTE]

To learn more about why we create evidence files, see Chapter 4.

7. RECORD.

1. Take a picture of the wall or whiteboard to capture all your hypotheses. This can serve as your backup if the wall gets erased.

2. Tabulate all your hypotheses in a document, such as an Excel or OneNote file. This document can serve as your team's backlog.

3. If you created a backlog of Customer hypotheses, in the previous Customer playbook, update your backlog with any newly generated customer and problem hypotheses.

Formulating a Discussion Guide

Here you will find sample questions to ask during your experiment. By including questions in your guide about [types of customers] and [job-to-be-done], you'll be able to verify that you're talking with your target customer and capture the [problems] they're experiencing.

Edit the guide to include the [parameters] you defined in your Problem hypotheses. Use these questions to get started, and then revise or create new questions if necessary.

1. FORMULATE QUESTIONS THAT VALIDATE [TYPES OF CUSTOMERS].

- What is your work environment like (e.g., size, physical surroundings, process maturity)?

- What are some of the key marketplace trends that your company faces?

- What things about your work environment would you characterize as being typical of other companies, and what things would you say are unique or exceptional?

- What is your job title and what are your primary responsibilities at your company?

- As a [type of customers], what high-level jobs/tasks do you perform?

- As a [type of customers], what kind of skills, experiences, and personal characteristics do you need?

- As a [type of customers], what platforms, tools, and technologies do you work with?

- As a [type of customers], what other types of people do you work with?

- As a [type of customers] what types of applications or services do you currently work on?

2. FORMULATE QUESTIONS THAT VALIDATE [JOB-TO-BE-DONE].

- When doing [job-to-be-done], what are some of the specific jobs/ tasks you perform?

- How often are you personally involved in [job-to-be-done]?

- Who is involved in [job-to-be-done] at your company?

- Tell me about how you do [job-to-be-done] today.

- Is there anything specific that you typically do before or after you do [job-to-be-done]?

- Are there multiple starting points for [job-to-be-done]? If so, what are they?

- What products, services, or technologies do you or others at your company currently use when doing [job-to-be-done]?

- Tell me about the last time you did [job-to-be-done].

- What were the major problems/challenges you faced when doing [job-to-be-done]?

3. FORMULATE QUESTIONS THAT VALIDATE [PROBLEM].

- What's your biggest frustration with [job-to-be-done]?

- Were there things that you were lacking that you needed when attempting [job-to-be-done]?

- When doing [job-to-be-done], what tools or workarounds have you used to get around [problem]?

- How well do these workarounds address the [problem]?

- How much time, effort, and money have you spent trying to work around [problem]?

- When you are attempting [job-to-be-done], what are the "little things" that frustrate you? Do these things happen frequently? How often?

- When you are attempting [job-to-be-done], what are the "big things" that happen infrequently but are problematic when they do happen?

- Have you experienced a problem that stopped you from being able to complete [job-to-be-done]? Can you tell me what happened?

- On a scale of 0–10 (where 10 is extremely affected), how affected are you by [problem]? Why?

- If we solved [problem], what would it allow you to achieve?

- If you could wave a magic wand and change anything about [job-to-be-done], what would it be?

4. FORMULATE QUESTIONS THAT EXPAND YOUR CUSTOMER FEEDBACK LOOP.

- Is there anyone else that I should also be talking with? Is there anyone you know who is experiencing [problem] when attempting [job-to-be-done]?

- May I contact you in the future if I have additional questions?

- In the future, if we had some early product ideas around [job-to-be-done], would that be something you'd be interested in seeing?

[NOTE]
To learn more about creating a shoebox, see Chapter 4.

5. DOCUMENT YOUR DISCUSSION GUIDE.

Once you have decided on the questions you want to ask during your interview, collect them into a document and store it in your shoebox for the team to refer to when conducting their experiment.

Experimenting

A key component to our customer-driven strategy is maintaining an ongoing conversation with your customers. One of the fastest and cheapest ways to collect rich customer data is to conduct direct, one-on-one interviews.

Preparing for the Interview

1. CREATE A SCREENER.

As a team, determine the questions that you'll use to ensure you're capturing the right customer for your study. Consider the following attributes for developing your screener:

- Work environment

- Job role

- Skills and job responsibilities

- Tools and technologies

- Jobs/tasks they perform

- The last time they performed the job/task

Here are some things to consider when creating your screener:

- Keep the screener short (5–10 questions).

- Remember that customers may try to align their answers to the attributes they think fit your study. Make sure that your questions don't make it obvious what type of candidate you're looking for.

- Once you begin the interview, you can ask some additional questions to ensure you have a customer that meets your target.

2. PREPARE A SCHEDULE.

A successful feedback loop should be organized and consistently flowing with customer interviews. Here are some things you should think about when scheduling customers for your interviews:

Date and time

Determine the schedule for your study based on your team's availability.

Duration

We recommend about 30 minutes, and no more than 60 minutes.

Location

Location options are in person, over the phone, or using video/voice conference systems (Microsoft Skype, Google Hangouts, or your own conferencing system).

Gratuity

You may consider offering a small gift for participating (gift card, free service, product giveaway, raffle for a prize, etc.).

Nondisclosure agreement (NDA)

Depending on the sensitivity of your discussion, you may have customers sign an NDA to protect your material.

Team members

Decide who will be included in the call (team members or other participants).

Recording

Determine if you would like to record the interview and what method you'll use.

Contact information

Provide details of how customers can get in contact with you regarding the interview.

Cancellation policy

Provide instructions on how a customer can cancel their appointment for their interview.

Special instructions

Provide any additional details (e.g., driving directions, how to connect to the video/voice chat).

[NOTE]
For more information about the roles used in an interview, see Chapter 3.

3. FIND CUSTOMERS.

Finding the right customer can be challenging. For tips on finding customers, see Chapter 3.

4. IDENTIFY ROLES.

You'll want to establish responsibilities for each team member before the interview. Here are some key roles you may want to establish:

Moderator

A single person to conduct the interview

Note taker

A person or multiple people to take notes, so the moderator can focus on conducting the interview

Timekeeper and logistical coordinator

A person to keep track of time and ensure equipment and other logistics are taken care of

5. CONDUCT A MOCK INTERVIEW.

Before engaging in customer conversations, you may want to practice your interview and refine your Discussion Guide.

It's helpful to conduct a "mock interview" with someone outside your immediate team. This will allow you to:

- Iterate on questions that were not clear, too complicated, or leading.

- Determine if your questions follow a natural flow.

- Test the length of your interview.

- Practice probing for more detailed information.

Conducting the Interview

A typical interview process breaks down into five steps:

1. SET UP (BEFORE INTERVIEW BEGINS).

MODERATOR: Review the Discussion Guide and prepare your space to remove any distractions.

NOTE TAKER: Create a place in the team's shoebox to keep all customer notes.

TIMEKEEPER/COORDINATOR: Sit next to the moderator so you can quietly update him or her on the amount of time remaining. If you're using a videoconferencing solution, make sure audio/video is working correctly.

2. MAKE THE INTRODUCTIONS (APPROXIMATELY 5 MINUTES).
MODERATOR:

1. Begin the introduction by welcoming the customer and thanking them for their willingness to participate in the study.

2. Introduce yourself and the team (the note takers and timekeeper).

3. Briefly describe the objectives of the interview.

4. Encourage the customer to be open and honest in their feedback. There are no right or wrong answers. Any information they provide will help you and the team learn. Even if their comments are negative, it will not hurt your feelings; it will only help you and the team develop better products.

5. Ask for permission to record the session.

NOTE TAKER: Record the date, time, and the team members that are participating in the call.

TIMEKEEPER/COORDINATOR: Once the interview begins, start the clock and begin tracking the time.

3. BREAK THE ICE (APPROXIMATELY 5 MINUTES).

MODERATOR: The first questions you ask the customer should be "ice-breakers," simple questions to make the customer feel comfortable.

You want to develop trust and rapport with the customer. You can do this by:

- Providing encouragement—making sure they know their feedback is valued.

- Being honest. Explain the purpose and intent of your study, and customers will be honest in return.

- Showing modesty. Explain that you are here to learn from their expertise.

- Being trustworthy—remind customers not to share anything confidential or proprietary.

Typically, asking the customer about their role at work, the applications/product they're developing, and the tools and technology they use are good warm-up questions.

NOTE TAKER: Try your best to capture everything the customer is saying. Do not paraphrase.

TIMEKEEPER/COORDINATOR: During the icebreaker questions, be sure the moderator keeps the conversation on track. Icebreaker questions can lead customers to tell you everything they think you want to know, going into their entire employment history and every project they've ever worked on. This can eat up a lot of time before you even get to the questions you care most about.

4. DISCUSS (APPROXIMATELY 15 MINUTES).

MODERATOR : Use the Discussion Guide to steer the conversation. Try to keep the tone casual, rather than reading off a script. This will become easier and more natural the more practice you have.

NOTE TAKER: Continue to capture as much as the customer says. You can use the Discussion Guide as a template for your responses. As best you can, don't paraphrase.

TIMEKEEPER/COORDINATOR: Signify to the moderator when they have reached a milestone (e.g., "10 minutes left," "5 minutes left," "1 more minute"). You can do this by writing on a notepad, sending a private IM, or passing a Post-it note.

5. WRAP UP (APPROXIMATELY 5 MINUTES).

MODERATOR:

1. Use this time to bring the conversation to an end. Ask any clarifying questions if necessary.

2. Open the call up to the team, allowing the note taker and timekeeper to ask questions.

3. Thank the customer for their time and feedback.

4. Provide gratuity for their time.

5. Ask for referrals—anyone they would recommend who would want to talk to you.

NOTE TAKER:

- Review your notes and determine if you need any more detail. When the Moderator opens the call, ask the customer any questions that can help clarify what you captured.

- When the notes are complete, be sure to include them in the team's Shoebox.

TIMEKEEPER/COORDINATOR:

1. Stop the recording.

2. Keep the recording in your team's shoebox.

Debriefing After Interviews

It's important to allocate time with the team, shortly after the interview, to give everyone a chance to share their insights or make suggestions for the next interview. Consider the following activities while debriefing:

- Capture meaningful information (direct quotes, surprising findings, context tools, etc.).

- Pull the most meaningful data, notes, pictures, direct customer quotes, frustrations, limitations, notable behaviors, or any other type of signal that validates or invalidates your hypotheses and place it in your team's evidence file.

- Consider gathering supportive customer evidence from online sources, such as their company logo, screenshots of their product, or even a picture of the customer from their LinkedIn profile. These materials will be beneficial later when you're creating the customer story to share with your organization.

Before the next interview, consider updating your interview materials based on your responses to the following questions:

- Was the customer the right fit? Do you need to update your screener to ensure you get the target customer?

- Did any of the questions need to be clarified or repeated? Is there a simpler way to ask the question? Should the question be broken up into smaller questions?

- Were any of the responses "off topic" or not in the area you were interested in? What was in the question that prompted this response?

- How long did each question take? Are you asking for too much detail? Too little detail?

- Was there enough time allocated to complete the Discussion Guide?

- Were there any technical issues that could have been avoided?

- Do the notes fully capture the conversation?

Sensemaking

Once the team has completed a series of interviews, it's time to interpret the customer's feedback.

As a team, work together to review all the interview notes and begin to make sense out of the data you've captured. Working together while analyzing data ensures that the team has a shared understanding about the conclusions that were made.

Schematizing the Data

1. PRINT OUT ALL YOUR INTERVIEW NOTES.

1. Return to your team's evidence file and print all interview notes.

   Through the playbook, we've encouraged documenting the outcome of each activity and placing it in your team's evidence file. It should now contain the most meaningful bits of data that comprise your point of view, vision, or strategy for your product.

   If you find that your evidence file is light and doesn't contain the data to validate or invalidate your hypotheses, go back to the shoebox and cull and organize the data you've collected along your journey and capture it in your evidence file.

2. Write a unique number or ID on the upper-right corner of each set of interview notes. This ID will allow you to relate the data you find to the specific customer.

3. Hand each team member one printed copy of an interview, a marker, and a stack of Post-it notes. Ideally, each team member should be reviewing notes from an interview conducted by someone other than themselves. This allows for a "second pair of eyes" and can often allow for multiple interpretations of the interview.

2. CAPTURE ANYTHING MEANINGFUL.

1. Thoroughly read the customer's interview notes.

2. When you find something meaningful, jot it down on a Post-it note. Here are some things you should be looking for:

   ○ Direct quotes

   ○ The customer's environment

   ○ Jobs they're performing

- Motivations

- Skills

- Tool use

- Expressed frustrations or limitations

- Delighters

Don't overthink it—write a sentence or two to capture your finding on a Post-it and then move on.

3. If you have multiple "types of customers" you've interviewed, capture their data on different colored Post-it notes. By color-coding the "types of customers," you'll be able to easily visualize them later in this activity.

3. TAG THE DATA.

Data tagging will allow your team to organize the data in an efficient way. Use Table 11-1 to get started. Feel free to modify it as necessary.

TABLE 11-1. Suggested tags for schematizing your data

TAG	TYPE OF FEEDBACK
Motivation	Comments that give you an indication of the customer's motivation
Frustration/problem	Statements or observations that indicate a problem, frustration, limitation, or constraint
Jobs-to-be-done	Actions or tasks that you observe customers are engaging in to achieve their goals
Attribute	Individual differences or characteristics that help define the customer
Interpersonal interaction	Communications or interactions you witnessed the customer having with another team member or client
Environment	Details that describe the context in which you observed the customer
Tool	Any tools that you witnessed your customer using to achieve their goals

Using these tags, determine the nature of the customer data point that you captured and write it in the upper-right corner of your Post-it note. For example, if the data point had something to do with the customer's frustration, it should be tagged with an "F." Additionally, write the customer ID from the interview on the upper-left corner of the Post-it note (see Figure 11-3).

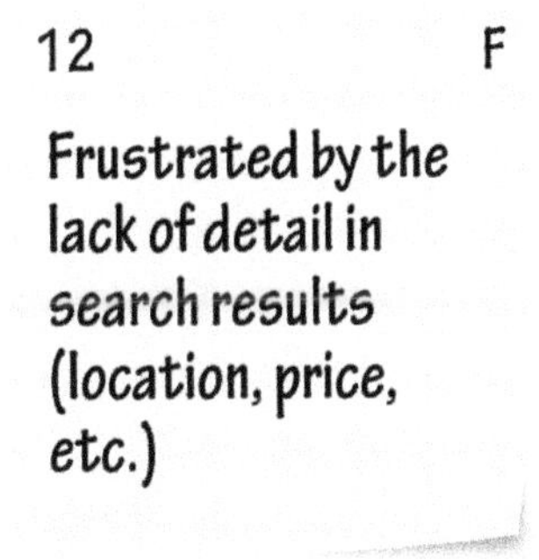

12   F

Frustrated by the lack of detail in search results (location, price, etc.)

FIGURE 11-3
A completed Post-it note for this exercise should be tagged with an interview ID (upper-left corner), a keyword tag (upper-right corner), and a brief description of the finding

Avoid the temptation of discussing the notes with the team. This gives each member enough time to focus on the interview notes, rather than discussing and comparing findings.

It also prevents the group from making premature conclusions before all the interviews have been reviewed. You'll get a chance to share your findings in the next step.

4. DISCUSS THE DATA.

Once the Post-it notes have been gathered on the wall, give your team a chance to discuss the customer interviews they read. Here are suggestions that can enrich the conversation:

1. Give each member time to talk about the customer they read about. Let them walk through what they learned and what stood out to them.

2. Other team members should ask questions to clarify what was learned. If the original interviewer or note taker is in the room, allow them to add further details that might not have been picked up in the notes.

3. Discuss if there is more to learn from the customer. If so, there may be an opportunity for the interviewer to call the customer back or email some follow-up questions.

5. ORGANIZE AND GROUP THE DATA.

You should start to notice some general themes or duplication. Organize the Post-it notes into groups or similarities (see Figure 11-4). Here are some suggestions to help make this a productive process:

- It's important to be flexible here. If someone on the team objects to combining a couple of items, don't force it. Just move on to more obvious pairings.

- Revise groups and rearrange notes until the team comes to an agreement.

- Look for patterns or gaps in your groupings and continue the discussion:

  ○ Which areas seem to have the largest groups? Frustrations? Motivations? Are there tags that are underrepresented? If so, were you asking the right questions to drive out those details?

  ○ Which items have the most duplication? Why was the team hearing that response frequently?

  ○ Is the same data frustration or motivation expressed in different words? What's the best way to summarize that learning?

  ○ Are there customer types that are underrepresented? Why are they not represented on the wall?

  ○ Are there common workarounds or tools used by customers?

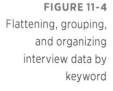

FIGURE 11-4
Flattening, grouping, and organizing interview data by keyword

Updating the Evidence File

Now that your team has spent time schematizing the data, update your evidence file. It should contain the most meaningful bits of data that comprise the team's customer observations, point of view, vision, and product strategy, including:

[NOTE]
For more information on the evidence file, see Chapter 4.

- Validated and invalidated hypotheses

- The notable things customers are saying, doing, thinking, and feeling in various contexts

- Problems, limitations, or frustrations customers experienced

- Customer quotes that exemplify a motivation, frustration, desire, or the like

- Customer behavior, work practices, tools or platforms they used, and so on

- Data points from external sources (market research, competitive analysis, etc.) that support your conclusions

Creating and Sharing Your Stories

After you've had time to interpret the data and discuss the learnings, you're ready to communicate your findings and vision. You can do that by telling a compelling story and determining a way to share it. To share the meaning of your data, you'll want to express it a way that others can easily understand.

Here are some examples of illustrative ways you can describe your data:

- Find a parallel or analogy that helps express the frustration your customers are having. Using an example that is outside your domain, but understood by everyone, can be a helpful way to take an abstract idea and make it more accessible to a broader audience.

- Draw diagrams or models that illustrate conflicting tensions (e.g., customers want high quality, but they also want to save money). Two-by-two tension models can help articulate these conflicts (see Figure 11-5).

- Create a timeline or journey map that shows the progression of a customer problem—how it starts out as a minor frustration but eventually leads to the customer opting out of the experience.

FIGURE 11-5

A two-by-two tension
model can help
illustrate the tensions
that occur when your
customer is making
decisions

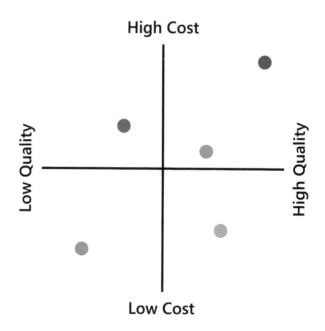

SHARE THE STORY

As customer advocates, share the information you've learned about your customers with your organization using the channels you've established as a team (standups, email alias, presentations, Slack channels, or newsletters).

In the Customer playbook, we recommend leveraging existing channels first, but also consider creating a physical visual display in a shared location. The materials, if curated well, will capture the organization's attention and get them interested in learning more. Take this opportunity to organize a meeting in the shared location. Invite teams to "walk the walls" with you while you describe the customer's journey and share the deep insights you learned along the way.

[12]

The Concept Playbook

Exploring Your Ideas Using a Concept Value Test

> We believe [concept] will solve [problem] and be valuable for [type of customer] when doing [job-to-be-done].
>
> We will know this to be true when we see [criteria].

This playbook is organized into three sections that align with the Customer-Driven Cadence:

Formulating

- Reframe customer problems/opportunities using "How might we?"

- Formulate problems and ideas into an idea map.

- Prioritize your ideas using the Impact/Effort Matrix.

- Turn ideas into fully articulated concepts and formulate a Concept hypothesis.

- Using storyboards, plot key experiences of your concept.

- Generate a Discussion Guide for talking with customers about your concept.

Experimenting

- Organize and prepare for your Concept Value Test.

- Conduct a Concept Value Test.

- Debrief after the Concept Value Test is complete and discuss what you've learned.

Sensemaking

- Use a structured method to derive patterns and meaning out of the results of your Concept Value Test.

- Define and communicate the principles of the concept.

Formulating

Formulating Ideas Using "How Might We?"

Once your team has identified and validated problems your customers are experiencing, you're ready to transition from customer to product development. As a team, you'll explore ways to take the problems you want to solve and reframe them using "How might we?"

1. SELECT YOUR MAIN PROBLEM.

1. Return to your evidence file where your validated problem hypotheses were captured.

2. Select one problem to begin working with.

3. Create the first level of the idea map by writing, "How might we solve [type of problem]?" on the wall or board. This is your main problem.

> How might we solve the lack of descriptive information
> on our service providers' profile pages?

Write this statement near the top of the board; you'll need the space below to fill in the idea map.

2. UNCOVER AND REFRAME UNDERLYING PROBLEMS.

1. For each response to your main problem, capture it on a Post-it note, starting the response with "HMW." Each response should continue the "How might we?" framing. These are your underlying problems (see Figure 12-1).

> HMW encourage service providers to add descriptive
> information to their profile page?

2. Post all HMW responses to the wall or board. This will create your second level of the idea map.

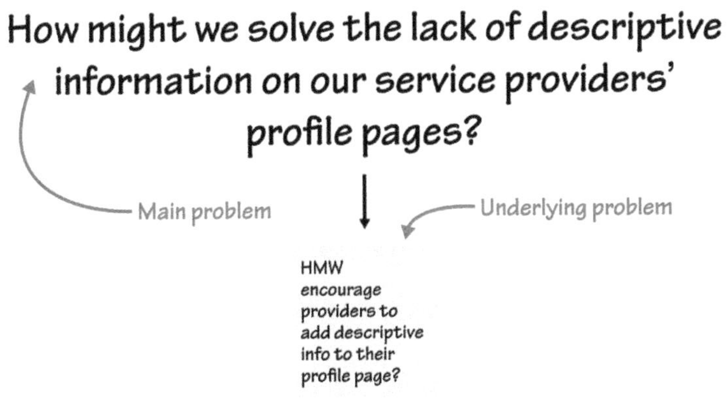

How might we solve the lack of descriptive information on our service providers' profile pages?

FIGURE 12-1

Using HMW to uncover an underlying problem

Main problem

Underlying problem

HMW encourage providers to add descriptive info to their profile page?

3. UNCOVER SMALLER, UNDERLYING PROBLEMS.

1. Identify one HMW response that the team formulated.

2. Ask the team "What's stopping the customer?" from achieving this idea.

   > What's stopping service providers from entering descriptive information about their business?

   The focus should be on what's stopping the customer from achieving the goal, not technical limitations of the product.

   > Service providers don't understand the benefit of updating their profile pages.

3. Continue to ask the team "What else?" until they've exhausted underlying blockers or problems. You should begin to identify problems that are smaller and more addressable.

   > Service providers are unaware that they can update their profile page.

   > Service providers don't know what information should go on their profile page.

   > Service providers don't see the benefits of updating their profile page.

   > Service providers forget to update their page when their business information changes.

4. Rephrase the underlying blockers into "How might we" statements and write each of them on its own Post-it note:

> HMW help providers understand the benefits of updating their page?

> HMW let providers know they can update their profile page?

> HMW help providers craft a descriptive profile page?

> HMW remind providers to update their profile page?

Hang these new notes next to each other under their parent problem. You should have created a branch that leads from the main problem to an underlying problem to a series of smaller underlying problems (see Figure 12-2).

FIGURE 12-2
Using HMW to uncover smaller, underlying problems

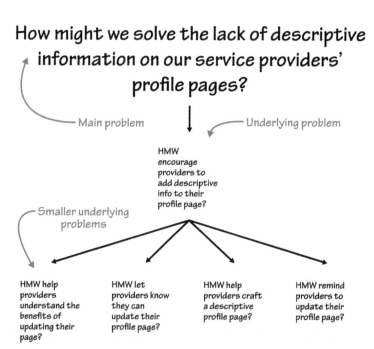

How might we solve the lack of descriptive information on our service providers' profile pages?

Main problem

Underlying problem

HMW encourage providers to add descriptive info to their profile page?

Smaller underlying problems

HMW help providers understand the benefits of updating their page?

HMW let providers know they can update their profile page?

HMW help providers craft a descriptive profile page?

HMW remind providers to update their profile page?

4. GENERATE IDEAS.

As a team, look at the subsequent "How might we" questions and respond with ideas. As you generate ideas, ask yourself:

- What are the different ways we could solve this problem?

- What barriers exist for the customer that prevents them from solving this problem?

- What's required of us to solve this problem?

- What do we need to do (as a team, division, or organization) to solve this problem?

5. RECORD.

1. Take a picture of the wall or whiteboard to capture the idea map.

2. Tabulate all ideas in a document, such as an Excel or OneNote file.

3. If possible, leave the idea map up so the team can further develop their ideas.

4. Keep the ideas generated in this activity in the team's shoebox.

5. For more information about creating a shoebox, see Chapter 4.

Prioritizing Your Ideas Using the Impact/Effort Matrix

Once your team has generated a list of possible ideas, you'll use the Impact/Effort Matrix to prioritize them. By prioritizing your ideas, you'll be able to identify the idea that you want to formulate a concept around.

1. CREATE THE IMPACT/EFFORT MATRIX.

1. To prepare for this activity, draw a 2×2 Impact/Effort Matrix.

2. Label the x-axis Effort (Low and High) and the y-axis Impact (Low and High).

3. Label the quadrants Long-term Strategy, Thankless Tasks, Pet Projects, and Quick Wins (starting in the High Impact/High Effort quadrant and moving clockwise, as shown in Figure 12-3).

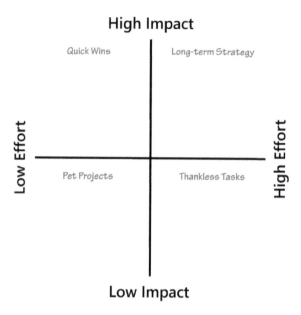

FIGURE 12-3

The Impact/Effort
Matrix with labeled
quadrants

High Impact

Quick Wins   Long-term Strategy

Low Effort   High Effort

Pet Projects   Thankless Tasks

Low Impact

2. SELECT AN IDEA.

1. Return to the shoebox, board, or wall where your team generated an idea map identifying a list of ideas.

2. Select one idea that the team has identified.

3. Answer the following questions about that idea:

    ○ How much effort will it take to implement this idea?

    ○ How much impact will this idea have on the customer?

    ○ How much impact will it have on the customer if we don't implement this idea?

4. Determine which quadrant on the Impact/Effort Matrix the idea belongs in.

5. Write the idea on a Post-it note and place it on the matrix.

3. REPEAT.

1. Proceed with this activity until the team has placed all the ideas on the Impact/Effort Matrix.

2. Stand back and evaluate the placement of ideas on the matrix.

3. Revise until the team comes to an agreement.

4. DISCUSS.

1. Review the placement of the ideas on the Impact/Effort Matrix and consider which ideas will result in the greatest impact for the customer.

2. Determine a prioritized list of ideas that the team will formulate concepts around.

5. RECORD.

1. Take a picture of the wall or board to capture the Impact/Effort Matrix.

2. Tabulate all ideas and their designated priority in a document, such as an Excel or OneNote file. This document will serve as your backlog.

3. Keep the backlog of ideas in the team's evidence file.

[NOTE]
For more information about creating a shoebox, see Chapter 4.

Turning Ideas into Concepts

Now that the team has prioritized their ideas, you'll want to formulate concepts. Concepts are well-articulated ideas that describe the unique value proposition, benefits, and limitations.

1. FORMULATE HYPOTHESES.

Write the Concept hypothesis on the wall or board large enough for the group to add Post-it notes to the [parameters].

> We believe [concept] will solve [problem] and be valuable for [type of customer] when doing [job-to-be-done].

> We will know this to be true when we see [criteria].

2. SELECT A [CONCEPT].

1. Return to the evidence file where the prioritized list of ideas was captured.

2. Select one idea that the team identified as a high priority. For the remainder of the activity, we'll refer to this idea as a concept.

3. Write the concept that your team selected on a Post-it note and place it on the [concept] parameter of the hypothesis written on the wall or board.

4. At this point in the HPF, you should have validated the [type of customers], [problem], and [job-to-be-done]. Capture those parameters on Post-it notes and place them on the hypothesis template to fill in the blank parameters.

The only new parameters at this stage are the [concept] and [criteria].

3. DEFINE [CRITERIA].

You'll need to define the criteria by which you will evaluate your concept's success. Measures such as need fulfillment, intent to use, believability, differentiation, and the willingness to recommend the concept to a friend or colleague are helpful criteria to measure the success of your concept.

1. As a team, review the following questions and rating scales. Use them to help you define your criteria. Modify the questions or add new criteria to fit your needs.

   ○ Would _____ solve a problem or fulfill a need for you?
     (Scale: "Definitely would not" (1) – (2) – (3) – (4) – (5) "Definitely would")

   ○ Assuming _____ would be available to you, would you use it?
     (Scale: "Definitely would not" (1) – (2) – (3) – (4) – (5) "Definitely would")

   ○ How believable is _____ as a solution?
     (Scale: "Not believable at all" (1) – (2) – (3) – (4) – (5) "Very believable")

   ○ How different is _____ from other solutions available?
     (Scale: "Not at all different" (1) – (2) – (3) – (4) – (5) "Very different")

   ○ How likely is it that you would recommend _____ to a friend or colleague?
     (Scale: "Definitely would not" (1) – (2) – (3) – (4) – (5) "Definitely would")

2. Using the Post-it notes, capture the criteria by which you will measure the success of your concept.

3. Place the Post-it notes on the [criteria] parameter of the hypothesis written on the wall or board.

4. You may have multiple criteria—that's expected. Write separate hypotheses for each criterion.

5. Before talking with customers, determine the score that you believe will qualify as success for your concept. Documenting the success metrics *before* you show your concept to customers will allow the team to remain objective when analyzing the results of the study.

Formulating the UVP, Benefits, and Limitations

1. FORMULATE THE UNIQUE VALUE PROPOSITION.

Formulate a unique value proposition ("elevator pitch") that best describes the overall value of the concept in two sentences or less.

1. Use the following questions to stimulate conversation with the team to generate the unique value proposition:

   - Who is this concept meant for?

   - What will the customer achieve by using this concept?

   - When will customers find this concept valuable (specific period, during a particular activity, job/task)?

   - Why should the customer care (saves them time, money, resources, etc.)?

   - How is it different than other solutions?

2. Allow each team member time to share their unique value proposition or "elevator pitch."

3. Work together to come up with a single value proposition that best describes your concept. Try to limit the pitch to two sentences.

4. Document the final unique value proposition.

2. FORMULATE CONCEPT BENEFITS.

Discuss the benefits of the concept. This is an opportunity to dig into the specific value the concept provides the customer.

1. For each of the following prompts, write your response on a Post-it note. You may have more than one response per prompt—that's expected! Capture one response per note.

   - With this concept, the customer can _____.

   - This concept does a good job at _____.

   - The customer will find this concept valuable because it _____.

2. Place each Post-it note on the wall or board. Don't overthink it. Fill up the wall with as many Post-it notes as possible.

3. Complete this part of the exercise individually. Later, you will have time to clarify what you've put on the wall.

4. Add duplicate notes. If one of your benefits is already on the wall, put yours up on the wall too. Duplication is a good thing! It means the team shares the same assumptions.

5. Look for overlap or duplication of benefits. Group those benefits together.

3. CONVERGE ON BENEFITS.

1. As a team, reduce the list to four to six benefits.

2. When you're considering the "cutline," think about the minimum number of benefits that you can include in the concept while still providing value to the customer.

3. Once you've whittled the list down to four to six benefits, write a simple one-sentence description of the specific value this benefit will provide the customer.

4. Document the benefits that your team has defined.

4. FORMULATE CONCEPT LIMITATIONS.

You're now going to focus on identifying the limitations of your concept. This is an opportunity to be transparent with customers and explain what the concept *won't* do.

1. For each of the following prompts, write your response on a Post-it note. You may have more than one response per prompt—that's expected! Capture one response per note.

   - The customer can't _____ with this concept.

   - When customers begin to use this concept, they won't be able to _____.

   - Customers may be frustrated by the lack of _____.

   - Due to technical limitations, the customer won't be able to _____.

2. Place each Post-it note on the wall or board. Don't overthink it. Fill up the wall with as many Post-it notes as possible.

3. Complete this part of the exercise individually. Later, you will have time to clarify what you've put on the wall.

4. Add duplicate notes. If one of your limitations is already on the wall, put yours up on the wall too. Duplication is a good thing! It means the team shares the same assumptions.

5. Look for overlap or duplication of limitations and group them together.

5. CONVERGE ON LIMITATIONS.

1. Reduce the list down to four to six limitations.

2. When you're considering the "cutline," think about the impact it will have on the value the concept provides the customer. Will you still be able to achieve the MVP if this limitation is present?

3. Once you've whittled the list down to four to six limitations, write a simple one-sentence description of how the customer will be affected by these limitations or constraints.

4. Document the limitations your team has defined.

6. RECORD.

1. Take a picture of the wall or whiteboard to capture all your hypotheses. This can serve as your backup if the wall gets erased.

2. If you created a backlog of Customer and Problem hypotheses in the previous playbooks, update it with your newly generated concept hypotheses. The hypotheses should be stored in your team's evidence file.

3. Capture the benefits, limitations, and unique value proposition in a document and store it in your shoebox for the team to refer to when conducting their experiment.

[NOTE]
To learn more about why we create a shoebox and evidence files, see Chapter 4.

Plotting Events Using Storyboards

Storyboarding can be an effective tool to help illustrate the experience a customer will have with your concept. The story of your concept can take shape over a three-frame storyboard. These three frames, or *keyframes*, highlight a pivotal moment in the experience. For example, you may use a storyboard to show the experience of your concept before it's introduced, during its use, and after the customer finishes using your concept.

A storyboard template is available at *customerdrivenplaybook.com* to help you get started.

1. DEFINE THE KEYFRAMES.

The keyframes are the three fundamental events in the customer's journey (i.e., before, during, and after). You can always add more frames if you need to.

1. In the first frame, describe the beginning of the story, the customer, and the problem they're experiencing performing a job/task.

2. As a team discuss what should be included in the first keyframe. Use the following questions as prompts to stimulate the conversation:

   - Who is the customer?

   - What are their motivations?

   - What is their work environment like (e.g., size, physical surroundings, process maturity)?

   - What job/task are they trying to accomplish?

   - What problems do they encounter when performing the job/task?

   - How do they feel when they have this problem?

   - What do they do in response to this problem?

3. In the second keyframe, capture how the team's concept will solve that problem. As a team, discuss what should be included in the second keyframe. Use the following questions as prompts to stimulate the conversation:

   - What problem is this concept solving?

   - How does the user feel when they use this concept?

   - How does this concept change their behavior?

   - What can the customer do with this concept that they couldn't before?

4. The third frame should capture the end of the story, the outcome the user will achieve by using the team's concept. Discuss what should be included in the third keyframe. Use the following questions as prompts to stimulate the conversation:

    ○ What does the customer accomplish while using this concept?

    ○ Has this concept alleviated their problem or limitation?

    ○ How do they feel when they reach their goal/outcome?

2. SKETCH THE KEYFRAMES.

Using the storyboard template provided on our website (*customer drivenplaybook.com*), capture the three keyframes. Under each keyframe, the story describes what's occurring in the storyboard (see Figure 12-4).

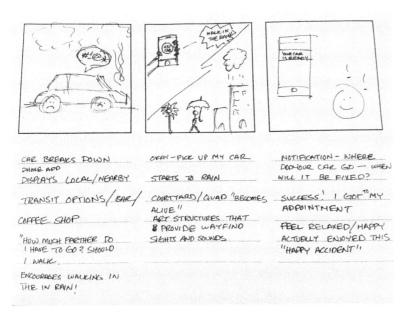

FIGURE 12-4

Storyboard using three keyframes: before, during, and after

3. DISCUSS.

1. Review the storyboard and consider:

    ○ Do the keyframes of the storyboard capture the customer's journey?

    ○ Does each keyframe tell a clear story about what the customer was experiencing before they used your concept, during, and after?

- Does the storyboard align with the concept's unique value proposition, benefits, and limitations?

2. Discuss the storyboard and iterate until the team has come to agreement on the final story.

[NOTE]

To learn more about why we create evidence files, see Chapter 4.

4. RECORD.

1. Take a picture of the wall or whiteboard to capture all your hypotheses. This can serve as your backup if the wall gets erased.

2. Tabulate all your hypotheses in a document, such as an Excel or OneNote file. This document can serve as your team's backlog.

3. If you created a backlog of Customer hypotheses in the previous Customer playbook, update your backlog with any newly generated customer and problem hypotheses.

Formulating a Discussion Guide for Talking with Customers

Here you will find questions to help guide your conversation with customers; you can use these questions to get started, and then revise or create new ones if necessary. The first sets of questions should be used at the beginning of the experiment, before you introduce the concept, to determine if you're talking with the target customer and if they're experiencing the problem you're trying to solve. After you've introduced and explored the concept with the customer, use the second set of questions to validate or invalidate that the concept solves a problem the customer is experiencing in a valuable way.

Before you introduce the concept, ask the following questions.

1. FORMULATE QUESTIONS THAT VALIDATE [TYPES OF CUSTOMERS].

- As a [type of customers] what high level jobs/tasks do you perform?

- As a [type of customers] what kind of skills, experiences, and personal characteristics do you need?

- As a [type of customers] what platforms, tools, and technologies do you work with?

2. FORMULATE QUESTIONS THAT VALIDATE [JOB-TO-BE-DONE].

- Tell me about the last time you did [job-to-be-done].

- What were the major problems/challenges you faced when doing [job-to-be-done]?

3. FORMULATE QUESTIONS THAT VALIDATE [PROBLEM].

- What's your biggest frustration with [job-to-be-done]?

- Is [problem] a challenge for you?

- On a scale of 0–10 (where 10 is extremely affected), how affected are you by [problem]? Why?

4. FORMULATE QUESTIONS THAT VALIDATE [CONCEPT].

Use the following questions, or a modified version, after you've introduced the concept.

- How important is this [concept]?

- How well would [concept] solve a problem or fulfill a need for you?

- How different is [concept] from other solutions currently available?

- Are you using a solution that's like [concept]? If so, how satisfied are you with it?

- Is there anything that [concept] does a good job at?

- Is there anything that [concept] does a bad job at?

- What are your overall thoughts about [concept]?

- When you think of other products like [concept], what are they good at?

- When you think of other products like [concept], what are they not as good at?

- How valuable is [concept]? Why do you feel that way?

- If [concept] were available to you today, would you use it?

- At what times would you use [concept]?

- In what ways would you use [concept]?

- Assuming [concept] were available on your job, would you download the trial today?

- How do you feel about buying/recommending/subscribing to a product or service that provided [concept]?

- Would you recommend [concept] to a friend or colleague?

[NOTE]

For more information
about creating
a shoebox, see
Chapter 4.

5. DOCUMENT YOUR QUESTIONS.

Once you have decided on the questions you want to ask during your discussion with customers, collect them into a document and store it in your shoebox for the team to refer to as needed.

Experimenting

Concept Value Tests (CVTs) allow customers to evaluate your early thinking, give feedback, and help assess whether you're presenting enough value with your concept. The CVT helps you identify the characteristics of your minimum viable product (MVP).

Preparing for the Concept Value Test

1. CREATE A SCREENER.

As a team, determine the questions that you'll use to ensure you're capturing the right customer for your study. Consider the following attributes for developing your screener:

- Work environment

- Job role

- Skills and job responsibilities

- Tools and technologies

- Jobs/tasks they perform

- The last time they performed the job/task

Here are some things to consider when creating your screener:

- Keep the screener short (5–10 questions).

- Remember that customers may try to align their answers to the attributes they think fit your study. Make sure that your questions don't make it obvious what type of candidate you're looking for.

- Once you begin the study, you can ask some additional questions to ensure you have a customer that meets your target.

2. PREPARE A SCHEDULE.

While preparing your schedule, consider the following topics:

Date and time

Determine the schedule for your study based on your team's availability.

Duration

We recommend between 30–60 minutes to conduct the study.

Location

Location options include in person or using video/voice conference systems (Microsoft Skype, Google Hangouts, or your own conferencing system).

Gratuity

You may consider offering a small gift for participating (gift card, free service, product giveaway, raffle for a prize, etc.).

Nondisclosure agreement (NDA)

Depending on the sensitivity of your discussion, you may have customers sign an NDA to protect your material.

Team members

Decide who will be included in the study (team members or other participants).

Recording

Determine if you would like to record the study and what method you'll use.

Contact information

Provide details of how customers can get in contact with you regarding the study.

Cancellation policy

Provide instructions on how a customer can cancel their appointment.

Special instructions

Provide any additional details (e.g., driving directions, how to connect to the video/voice chat).

3. FIND CUSTOMERS.

Finding the right customer can be challenging. For tips on finding customers, see Chapter 3.

4. IDENTIFY ROLES.

[NOTE]

For more information about the roles, see Chapter 3.

Here are some key roles you may want to establish before the study:

Moderator

A single person to conduct the CVT

Note taker

A person or multiple people to take notes, so the moderator can focus on conducting the CVT

Timekeeper/logistical coordinator

A person to keep track of time and ensure equipment and other logistics are taken care of

5. ORGANIZE YOUR MATERIALS.

During the formulating activities, you generate a lot of materials to create a fully articulated concept. To prepare for the experiment, you'll need to pull those materials together to present your concept to customers.

Use the Microsoft PowerPoint template, which can be found on our website (*customerdrivenplaybook.com*), to communicate the concept with customers. This template will provide you with a structured way to share the following materials:

- Unique value proposition
- Storyboards
- Concept benefits
- Concept limitations
- Rating scales

In addition to the template, you'll want to have the Discussion Guide available to ensure that you capture all the questions and topics you'll need to test your hypotheses.

Conducting the Concept Value Test

A Concept Value Test breaks down into five steps:

1. SET UP (BEFORE THE CVT BEGINS).

MODERATOR: Print and review the Discussion Guide. Prepare your space to remove any distractions. Make sure you have the CVT template completed and ready to share (in person or using video/voice conference systems).

NOTE TAKER: Create a place in the team's shoebox to keep all customer notes.

TIMEKEEPER/COORDINATOR: Sit next to the moderator so you can quietly update him or her on the amount of time remaining. If you're using a video-conferencing solution, make sure audio/video is working correctly. If you're planning on presenting the concept to the customer, using presentation software, make sure all equipment used to present is working.

2. MAKE THE INTRODUCTIONS(APPROXIMATELY 5 MINUTES).

MODERATOR:

1. Begin the introduction by welcoming the customer and thanking them for their willingness to participate in the study.

2. Introduce yourself and the team (the note takers and timekeeper).

3. Briefly describe the objectives of the study.

4. Encourage the customer to be open and honest in their feedback. There are no right or wrong answers. Any information they provide will help you and the team learn. Even if their comments are negative, it will not hurt your feelings; it will only help you and the team develop better products.

5. Ask for permission to record the session.

NOTE TAKER: Record the date, time, and the team members that are participating in the study.

TIMEKEEPER/COORDINATOR: Once the study begins, start the clock and begin tracking the time.

3. BREAK THE ICE (APPROXIMATELY 10 MINUTES).
MODERATOR:

- The first questions you ask the customer should be "icebreakers," simple questions to make the customer feel comfortable.

- Typically, asking the customer about their role at work, the applications/product they're developing, or the tools and technology they use are good warm-up questions.

- Use the Discussion Guide to steer the conversation. You should include questions that cover the following topics: [type of customers], [job-to-be-done], and [problem].

- Try to be conversational, rather than reading off a script. This will become easier and more natural the more practice you have.

NOTE TAKER: Capture as much of the customer's feedback as possible. You can use the Discussion Guide as a template for your responses. As best you can, don't paraphrase.

TIMEKEEPER/COORDINATOR: Signify to the moderator when they have reached a milestone (e.g., "10 minutes left," "5 minutes left," "1 more minute") You can do this by writing on a notepad, sending a private IM, or passing a Post-it note.

4. CONDUCT THE CONCEPT VALUE TEST (APPROXIMATELY 40 MINUTES).
MODERATOR: Present the unique value proposition and storyboard. Present the "elevator pitch" and walk the customer through your storyboard (if you have one):

1. Introduce the concept by sharing a simple description of the concept, the "elevator pitch."

2. Optionally, use the storyboard alongside the elevator pitch to help convey the function, value, or utility of the concept.

3. Allow the customer time to think about the concept you're exploring, remembering that they're seeing the concept for the first time.

4. Ask the customer to provide feedback on the concept.

5. If the customer responds, "I'd need to know more," ask them what questions they have at this point. You don't need to jump ahead and provide details, just capture what they would expect the concept to do, how it should behave, and what value it provides, if any.

6. Determine if the customer is confused. If so, explore what confuses them. You may need to update your elevator pitch for the next participant if it is not clear.

5. PRESENT THE BENEFITS.

1. Explain that the concept has multiple benefits, but that you're going to reveal them one at a time.

2. After each benefit, pause and ask the customer if the benefit is important to them and why.

3. Ask the customer to rank the benefits from most impactful to least impactful.

4. Once they've ranked the benefits, ask them why they ranked them in that order.

6. PRESENT THE LIMITATIONS.

1. Explain to the customer that the concept also has limitations that you would like to explain, revealing them one at a time.

2. After each limitation, pause and ask the customer if the limitation impacts them and how.

3. Ask the customer to rank the limitations from most impactful to least impactful.

4. Once they've ranked the limitations, ask them why they ranked them in that order.

5. Ask the customer which, if any, of the limitations would prevent them from using the concept as a solution.

7. PRESENT THE RATING SCALES.

1. Explain to the customer that you'd like them to provide feedback on the overall concept, considering the benefits and limitations.

2. Ask the rating questions that you've captured in your Discussion Guide.

NOTE TAKER:

1. Capture, as much as possible, all customer feedback on the benefits and limitations.

2. List, in order, the rankings the customer provides for benefits and limitations.

TIMEKEEPER/COORDINATOR:

1. Signify to the moderator when they have reached a milestone or if they are spending too much time on a topic, and encourage them to move forward.

2. Provide any technical support the moderator or customer may need.

3. Make sure that the recording is still running.

8. WRAP UP (APPROXIMATELY 5 MINUTES).

MODERATOR:

1. Use this time to review the Discussion Guide and ask any [concept] questions.

2. Once you've covered all the Discussion Guide topics, bring the conversation to an end.

3. Open the call up to the team, allowing the note taker and time-keeper to ask questions.

4. Thank the customer for their time and feedback.

5. Provide gratuity for their time (optional).

6. Ask for referrals—anyone they would recommend who would want to talk to you.

NOTE TAKER:

1. Review the Discussion Guide and see if you've captured responses for all topics. Read over your notes to determine if you need any more detail.

2. When the moderator opens the call, ask the customer any questions that can help clarify what you captured.

3. When the notes are complete, be sure to include them in the team's shoebox.

TIMEKEEPER:

1. Stop the recording.

2. Keep the recording in your team's shoebox or another shared location.

Debriefing After the Concept Value Test

It's important to allocate time with the team, shortly after the Concept Value Test, to give everyone a chance to share their insights and make suggestions for updates or iterations necessary for the next CVT. During the debrief you'll want to:

- Capture all meaningful information (direct quotes, surprising findings, context tools, etc.).
- Keep everything in the shoebox for safekeeping and future reflection.
- Pull the most meaningful data, notes, pictures, direct customer quotes, or any other type of signal that validates or invalidates your hypotheses and place it in your team's evidence file.

Here some things the team can discuss during their debriefing:

- Did the customer experience the problem that the concept was intended to solve?
- Did the customer understand the elevator pitch? Did it convey the overall value of the concept?
- Did the storyboard help visualize the value of the concept? Do adjustments need to be made?
- Were the benefits and limitations of the concept clearly understood?
- Did the customer find any of the limitations "dealbreakers," reducing their willingness to use the concept?
- Were any of the benefits considered "not valuable" to the customer? Why?

Sensemaking

Once the team has completed a series of Concept Value Tests, it's time to interpret the customer's feedback to determine if the concept is solving the right problem for them.

Work together to review the data, extract meaningful information, determine the "must have" functionality, and communicate the findings.

Schematizing the Data

1. CALCULATE AND QUALIFY RATING SCORES.

1. Return to your team's shoebox and review the Concept Value Test notes.

2. Calculate the rating scores you used to measure the overall value of the concept (need fulfillment, intent to use, believability, etc.).

3. Before talking with customers, you determined the score that you believe will qualify as success for your concept. Review the customer's final scores and determine which scores met your criteria.

4. If you used the sample questions provided, you should be able to answer the following questions about your concept:

   - Would this concept solve a problem the customer is experiencing today?

   - Would customers try the concept today, if it were available?

   - Would customers be willing to recommend the concept to a friend or colleague?

   - Does the customer find the concept unique and different from what's already available?

5. Capture your results in a document and save it to the team's evidence file.

2. CAPTURE QUALITATIVE FEEDBACK.

1. Thoroughly read the CVT notes. In addition to the quantitative measures, customers should have provided qualitative feedback on the concept.

2. When you find something meaningful, jot it down in a document. Here are some things you should be looking for:

- Direct quotes

- Feedback that validates or invalidates your Concept hypothesis

- Comments about value or differentiation

- Statements about time, cost, or resource savings

- References to efficiency, reduction in steps, or faster process

- Skepticism about the product

- Statements that the concept will solve a problem or fulfill a need

Listen for red flag responses like "I wouldn't use this concept, but I see how it could be useful for others," "It doesn't solve a problem I have right now, but maybe in the future," or "I have a solution similar to this, but maybe I'd start using this concept."

If you're hearing customers express those sentiments, the concept is not solving the right problem for them.

3. CALCULATE BENEFIT RANKINGS.

1. Tabulate all customers' rankings of the benefits from "most impactful" to "least impactful."

2. Take note of feedback customers provided about each benefit. Feedback to look for:

- What's the most valuable benefit the concept offers, if any?

- What benefits are essential to fulfill the customer's needs?

- Do any of the benefits or a combination of benefits elevate or reduce the problem?

- Were there any benefits mentioned that you were unaware of?

3. Capture your results in a document and save it to the team's Evidence File.

4. CALCULATE LIMITATION RANKINGS.

1. Tabulate the customers' ranking of the limitations in order of "most impactful" to "least impactful."

2. Take note of any feedback on the impact it has on the concept, if any. Feedback to look for:

   ○ What's the most impactful limitation, if any? Will the customer refuse to use the concept if this limitation exists?

   ○ Based on your understanding from customer comments, which limitations could remain but still keep the concept viable?

   ○ Were there any limitations that customers saw as a benefit? Is there a way to treat the limitation as a feature benefit?

   ○ Were there any limitations mentioned that you were unaware of?

3. Capture your results in a document and save it to the team's evidence file.

Determining "Must Have" Benefits

You can prioritize the concept by organizing the functionality provided in the benefits and limitations into three categories: must have, nice-to-have, and unnecessary features.

Start with the quantitative scores, but use the qualitative data to inform the team's decision on the category placement.

1. ORGANIZE THE DATA.

1. Using the large Post-it notes, write one category per note (must have, nice-to-have, and unnecessary).

2. Post the notes on the wall or board.

2. CATEGORIZE THE BENEFITS.

1. Return to your shoebox and pull out the benefits ranking.

2. Write each benefit on a small Post-it note.

3. As a team, determine which of the three categories each benefit should be placed in (Figure 12-5).

4. As a rule of thumb, if a benefit was ranked:

   - At the top of the list, "most impactful," consider putting it in the "must have" category.

   - In the middle of the list, consider putting it in the "nice-to-have" category.

   - Toward the bottom of the list, "least impactful," consider putting it in the "nice-to-have" or "unnecessary" category.

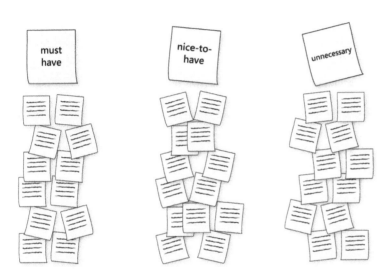

FIGURE 12-5
A team hanging Post-it notes under the three categories "must have," "nice-to-have," and "unnecessary"

3. CATEGORIZE THE LIMITATIONS.

1. Return to your shoebox and pull out the rankings of the limitations.

2. Write each limitation on a small Post-it note.

3. As a team, determine which of the three categories each limitation should be placed in.

4. Consider the impact the limitation will have on the concept:

   - If it's ranked "most impactful" or a "dealbreaker," consider adding it to the "must have" category.

   - If it had little impact or no impact (middle or bottom of the list), consider putting it in the "unnecessary" category.

4. TURN YOUR MUST HAVES INTO DESIGN PRINCIPLES.

Before moving to the next stage of product development, consider turning your must haves into a set of design, functionality, or interaction principles. As you begin to design the features that will bring your concept to life, it will help your team to continually reflect on the principles as a guide of what was critically important to the customer.

[NOTE]

For more information on the evidence file, see Chapter 4.

Updating the Evidence File

Now that your team has spent time schematizing the data, update your evidence file. It should contain the most meaningful bits of data that comprise the team's point of view, vision, and product strategy, including:

- Validated and invalidate hypotheses

- Design principles or categorized features

- Customer quotes that exemplify a motivation, frustration, desire, or the like

- Data points from external sources (market research, competitive analysis, etc.) that support your conclusions

- Models, diagrams, or illustrations that help communicate your findings

Creating and Sharing Your Stories

At this point, you're either celebrating that you've found a concept that solves the problem in a way that your customers find valuable, or thankful that you didn't spend countless hours and resources developing a product customers won't use. Either way, you should consider the experiment a success!

Now it's time to share what you've learned with your organization. To share the meaning of your data, you'll want to express it a way that others can easily consume and understand.

Some examples of illustrative ways you can describe your data:

- Convey a set of design, functionality, or interaction principles that will bring your concept to life; it will help your team to continually reflect on the principles as a guide of what was critically important to the customer.

- Use heat maps to represent customer responses to the rating scales. Illustrations using simple red and green color schemes to convey meaning allow the audience to quickly comprehend the customer's reaction to your concept.

- Create a timeline or journey map that shows the progression of a customer problem and how the concept saves them time, steps, or frustration and leads to the customer having a desirable experience. Use customer quotes along with their behaviors to emphasize their feelings of delight, frustration, anxiety, and so on (see Figure 12-6).

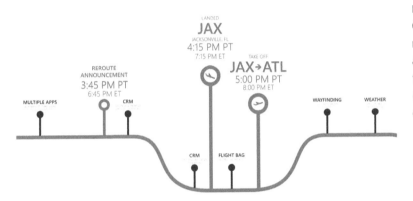

FIGURE 12-6

Customer journey map showing how an airline will interact with various applications during a traveler's experience

SHARE THE STORY

You've invested heavily in learning about your customers and their problems, and now you have a concept that solves their problems in a way customers find valuable. You should shout it from the rooftops! If that doesn't work, share your learning with your organization using the channels you've established as a team (standups, email alias, presentations, Slack channels, or newsletters).

In the Customer playbook, we recommended flattening out the data and displaying it in a shared location. By continuously sharing your learnings, you not only increase your understanding of the customers, but also raise the organization's customer IQ.

As you continue to learn more about your customers, you'll want to keep the display materials fresh and updated. By displaying illustrations such as mockups/prototypes, heat maps, timelines, or journey maps, you'll grab the attention of your organization and keep them heavily invested in learning about the customer's journey.

[13]

The Feature Playbook

Testing Your Features
Using a Usability Study

> We believe that [type of customers] will be successful solving
> [problem] using [feature] while doing [job-to-be-done].
>
> We will know they were successful when we see [criteria].

This playbook is organized into three sections that align with the
Customer-Driven Cadence:

Formulating

- Formulate your "must have" benefits into features that can be
  tested with customers.

- Fully articulate Feature hypotheses with measurable criteria.

- Create tasks that represent the expected workflow.

- Generate a Discussion Guide for walking customers through your
  usability study and asking them questions about their experience.

Experimenting

- Prepare for your usability study.

- Test features with customers using prototypes (clickable mockups).

- Debrief after the usability study and discuss what you've learned.

Sensemaking

- Use a structured method to derive patterns and meaning from the
  results of your usability study.

- Share your insights with your organization.

Formulating

Formulating Benefits into Features

During the Concept stage, you validated that you were solving the problem in a way that customers found valuable—determining that you were in fact building *the right thing*.

In the Feature stage, you'll turn the concept benefits into a collection of features to deliver on the minimum viable product (MVP)—testing that you're building the concept *the right way*.

1. SELECT YOUR "MUST HAVE" CONCEPT BENEFITS.

1. Return to your evidence file where your categorized list of concept benefits were captured.

2. Review your concept's unique value proposition, benefits, and limitations.

3. Select the "must have" benefits; these were the benefits that customers found "most impactful."

4. Using medium Post-it notes, write one benefit per note. Place the notes on the wall or board horizontally. These notes will serve as your column labels.

2. GENERATE FEATURES THAT DELIVER ON THE BENEFITS.

1. As a team, brainstorm and generate multiple feature ideas. These are the features you believe your team could build to deliver each benefit.

2. For each of the "must have" benefits, capture as many features as you can think of on Post-it notes. Capture one response per note and place it under the appropriate benefit.

3. Don't worry about the time or resources it may take to deliver on features; you'll address that later. Right now, your goal is to brainstorm and generate multiple feature ideas.

Prioritizing the Feature Work Using the Impact/Effort Matrix

1. PREPARE THE IMPACT/EFFORT MATRIX.

In the previous activity, the focus was to diverge and generate multiple feature ideas for each benefit. Now, it's time to converge on the set of features to achieve your MVP.

Using the matrix, determine the amount of effort it will take your team to deliver each feature and the impact it will provide your customers.

1. To prepare for this activity, draw a 2×2 Impact/Effort Matrix.

2. Label the x-axis Effort (Low and High) and the y-axis Impact (Low and High).

3. Label the quadrants Long-term Strategy, Thankless Tasks, Pet Projects, and Quick Wins (starting in the High Impact/High Effort quadrant and moving clockwise, as shown in Figure 13-1).

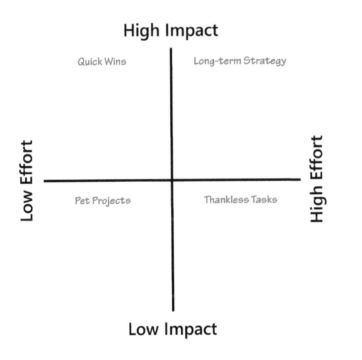

FIGURE 13-1
The Impact/Effort Matrix with labeled quadrants

2. SELECT A FEATURE.

1. Select one feature to begin.

2. As a team, discuss the following questions:

   - How much effort will it take to implement this feature?

   - How much impact will this feature have on the customer?

   - What's the risk if we don't implement this feature?

3. Determine which quadrant on the Impact/Effort Matrix the feature belongs in and hang it on the wall or board.

3. REPEAT.

1. Proceed with this activity until the team has placed all features on the Impact/Effort Matrix.

2. Stand back and evaluate the placement of features on the matrix.

3. Revise until the team comes to an agreement.

4. DISCUSS.

1. Review the placement of the features on the Impact/Effort Matrix.

2. Discuss the priority of the work and the features necessary to achieve the MVP. You may need to include other resources, such as engineering schedules and product timelines, to help you decide on the features you want to pursue.

5. RECORD.

1. Take a picture of the wall or board to capture the Impact/Effort Matrix.

2. Tabulate all features and their designated priority in a document, such as an Excel or OneNote file. Use this document as a backlog of feature ideas.

3. Keep the list of features and their priority in the team's evidence file.

Formulating Feature Hypotheses

As in the previous stages of development, before you begin to test features with customers, your team should formulate Feature hypotheses.

At this point, you should have most of the parameters defined and validated, including the type of customer, problem, and job-to-be-done. You'll just need to plug in your features and define the success metrics.

1. FORMULATE HYPOTHESES.

Write the Feature hypothesis on the wall or board large enough for the group to add Post-it notes to the [parameters].

> We believe that [type of customers] will be successful solving [problem] using [feature] while doing [job-to-be-done].

> We will know they were successful when we see [criteria].

2. SELECT A [FEATURE].

1. Return to the evidence file where the prioritized list of features was captured.

2. Select one feature and write it on a Post-it note. Place the note on the [feature] parameter of the hypothesis written on the wall or board.

3. DEFINE THE [CRITERIA].

As in the Concept stage, you'll use measurable criteria to define what it looks like when a customer is successful with your feature. The goal is to have criteria that allow the team to remain objective.

1. Using the Post-it notes, capture the criteria by which you will measure the success of your feature. Consider the following questions when determining your criteria:

   - How will you know when a customer has successfully used the feature?

   - How will you determine if the feature is simple to use?

   - What would customers say if they are satisfied or enjoy the feature?

- What type of behavior would customers display if they find your feature desirable?

- How will you know when customers understand what they're doing and why they're doing it?

2. Place the Post-it notes on the [criteria] parameter of the hypothesis written on the wall or board. You may have multiple criteria—that's expected. Write separate hypotheses for each criterion.

4. REPEAT.

1. Continue to articulate hypotheses for all features you want to include in your experiment.

2. Write all your hypotheses on the board or wall.

3. Stand back and evaluate the number of hypotheses that the team has generated.

4. Revise hypotheses until the team comes to an agreement.

[NOTE]
To learn more about evidence files, see Chapter 4.

5. RECORD.

1. Take a picture of the wall or whiteboard to capture all your hypotheses. This can serve as your backup if the wall gets erased.

2. Tabulate all your hypotheses in a document, such as an Excel or OneNote file. This document can serve as your team's backlog.

3. If you created a backlog of hypotheses in the previous playbooks, update your backlog with any newly generated hypotheses.

4. Keep all hypotheses in the team's evidence file.

[NOTE]
For more information about creating tasks, see Chapter 8.

Formulating Tasks

At the Feature stage, you'll define tasks that allow you to test the usability of your feature. Be sure that your tasks are:

Reasonable

Something you could reasonably expect a customer to do in everyday situations.

Achievable

"Solvable"—that is, they can be completed by the customer.

Specific

Detailed and descriptive. Avoid tasks that are vague and left to the customer's interpretation.

Sequential

The tasks should walk a customer through an entire workflow in order. Avoid "jumping around" doing tasks that are unassociated with each other.

Formulating a Testable Prototype

You'll need a way for customers to interact with your feature to complete the tasks you've given them. One way to achieve this is by creating a *prototype*.

Here are the most common forms of prototypes used during feature usability testing:

Sketches

Low-fidelity mockups are typically hand-drawn, but serve as a low-cost way to get your feature in front of customers. They're fast and allow for quick design iterations. However, you won't be able to test the nuances of the design interaction, workflow complexity, or responsiveness.

Wireframes

Static or dynamic (e.g., "clickable") wireframes bring a higher fidelity to the feature you're testing. Depending on the complexity, they can be costlier than low-fidelity sketches, but often allow your customer to experience a more realistic version of your feature.

Interactive prototypes

Prototyping your feature will provide the most realistic customer experience. You'll be able to capture the nuances of the design interaction, layout, navigation, and workflow of your feature. Depending on your team's level of coding or manufacturing skills, prototypes can be the costliest asset for feature usability testing.

Formulating a Discussion Guide

Feature testing isn't just about testing the success of your feature. It's an opportunity to continue to validate that you're targeting the right customer and solving a problem that they experience.

Just as in all the other stages of the HPF, you'll want to formulate questions that will guide your conversation with customers. Use these questions to get started, and then revise or create new questions if necessary. You'll ask these questions before and after the customer completes the usability test. The first set of questions will help you identify if you're talking to the target customer. After the study, the second set of questions will help you determine if the customer found the features usable.

Before you introduce the feature, ask the following questions.

1. FORMULATE QUESTIONS THAT VALIDATE [TYPES OF CUSTOMERS].

- As a [type of customers] what high-level jobs/tasks do you perform?

- As a [type of customers] what kind of skills, experiences, and personal characteristics do you need?

- As a [type of customers] what platforms, tools, and technologies do you work with?

2. FORMULATE QUESTIONS THAT VALIDATE [JOB-TO-BE-DONE].

- Tell me about the last time you did [job-to-be-done].

- What were the major problems/challenges you faced when doing [job-to-be-done]?

3. FORMULATE QUESTIONS THAT VALIDATE [PROBLEM].

- What's your biggest frustration with [job-to-be-done]?

- Is [problem] a challenge for you?

- On a scale of 0–10 (where 10 is extremely affected), how affected are you by [problem]? Why?

Use the following questions, or a modified version, after you've conducted the usability test.

4. FORMULATE QUESTIONS THAT VALIDATE [FEATURE].

- Would using this [feature] be useful in your job?

- Would using this [feature] make you more productive?

- Assuming this [feature] were available, would you use it on a regular basis?

- Do you think this [feature] would be easy to learn?

- Would you be satisfied using this [feature]?

- Would you recommend this [feature] to a friend or colleague?

5. FORMULATE QUESTIONS THAT VALIDATE USABILITY (USE QUESTIONNAIRE—ABBREVIATED).

1. It is simple to use.
   (Scale: "Strongly Disagree" (1) – (2) – (3) – (4) – (5) – (6) – (7) "Strongly Agree")

2. It is useful.
   (Scale: "Strongly Disagree" (1) – (2) – (3) – (4) – (5) – (6) – (7) "Strongly Agree")

3. It is fun to use.
   (Scale: "Strongly Disagree" (1) – (2) – (3) – (4) – (5) – (6) – (7) "Strongly Agree")

4. It does everything I would expect it to do.
   (Scale: "Strongly Disagree" (1) – (2) – (3) – (4) – (5) – (6) – (7) "Strongly Agree")

5. I learned to use it quickly.
   (Scale: "Strongly Disagree" (1) – (2) – (3) – (4) – (5) – (6) – (7) "Strongly Agree")

6. It would help me be more effective.
   (Scale: "Strongly Disagree" (1) – (2) – (3) – (4) – (5) – (6) – (7) "Strongly Agree")

6. DOCUMENT YOUR QUESTIONS.

Once you have decided on the questions to include in your Discussion Guide, collect them into a document and store it in your team's shoebox.

[NOTE]

For more information about creating a shoebox, see Chapter 4.

Experimenting

Preparing for the Usability Study

1. CREATE A SCREENER.

As a team, determine the questions that you'll use to ensure you're capturing the right customer for your study.

If you've already created a successful screener for any of the other stages of the HPF, reuse it to recruit customers that meet your criteria.

If this is the first time you're creating one, consider the following attributes for developing your screener:

- Work environment
- Job role
- Skills and job responsibilities
- Tools and technologies
- Jobs/tasks they perform
- The last time they performed the job/task

Here are some screening tips we've learned while recruiting customers:

- Keep the screener short (5–10 questions).
- Remember that customers may try to align their answers to the attributes they think fit your study. Make sure that your questions don't make it obvious what type of candidate you're looking for.
- Once you begin the study, you can ask some additional questions to ensure you have a customer that meets your target.

2. PREPARE A SCHEDULE.

Here are some things you should think about when scheduling customers for your study:

Date and time
Determine the schedule for your study based on your team's availability.

Duration
We recommend about 60 minutes, or 90 minutes at the most.

Location

Location options are an in-person lab study or remote testing using video/voice conference systems (Microsoft Skype, Google Hangouts, or your own conferencing system).

Gratuity

You may consider offering a small gift for participating (gift card, free service, product giveaway, raffle for a prize, etc.).

Nondisclosure agreement (NDA)

Depending on the sensitivity of your discussion, you may have customers sign an NDA to protect your material.

Team members

Decide who will be included in the study.

Recording

Determine if you would like to record the study and what method you'll use.

Contact information

Provide details of how customers can get in contact with you regarding the study.

Cancellation policy

Provide instructions on how a customer can cancel their appointment for the study.

Special instructions

Provide any additional details (e.g., driving directions, how to connect to the video/voice chat).

3. FIND CUSTOMERS.

Finding the right customer can be challenging. For tips on finding customers, see Chapter 3.

4. IDENTIFY ROLES.

Establish responsibilities for each team member before the study. Here are some key roles you may want to establish:

[NOTE]
For more information about the roles used in an interview, see Chapter 3.

Moderator

A single person to conduct the study

Note taker

A person or multiple people to take notes, so the moderator can focus on conducting the study

Timekeeper

A person to keep track of time and ensure equipment and other logistics are taken care of

Observers

Members of the team that want to listen and observe the usability test

Providing instructions on expected behavior for anyone joining the usability study will ensure a great experience for the team and the customer. Some things to consider:

- Encourage the team to close their laptops and completely focus on listening and observing the customer.

- If you're face-to-face with customers, allow only one additional team member to join the study. You don't want to intimidate the customer.

- If you're in a lab with a two-way mirror or conducting the study remotely, encourage the entire team to join, but remain silent until the moderator gives you an opportunity to provide feedback or ask questions.

5. CONDUCT A MOCK USABILITY STUDY.

Before conducting the usability study with customers, you may want to conduct a pilot study first. It's helpful to conduct a "dry run" with someone outside your immediate team. This will allow you to:

- Iterate on your questions, tasks, or instructions in your Discussion Guide that were not clear, too complicated, or leading.

- Ensure that the tasks follow a natural flow.

- Test the length of the study.

- Practice probing for more detailed information.

- Set up the equipment and make sure that it's working properly.

Conducting the Usability Study

A typical usability study (Figure 13-2) breaks down into five steps: setup, introduction, discussion, tasks, and wrap-up.

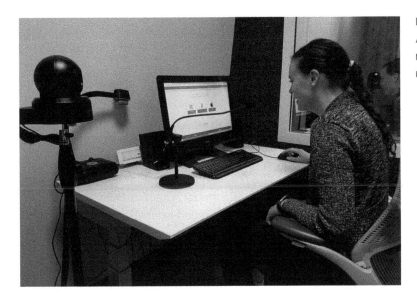

FIGURE 13-2
A participant being recorded during a usability study

1. SET UP (BEFORE THE USABILITY STUDY BEGINS).

MODERATOR: Review the Discussion Guide. Make sure you have the study materials ready to share (in-person lab study or remote testing). Depending on the location of your study, do your best to accommodate observers and ensure that they can see and hear the customer.

NOTE TAKER: Create a shared location for your notes. Tools like OneNote and Evernote are helpful in syncing notes across multiple devices.

TIMEKEEPER/COORDINATOR: Sit next to the moderator so you can quietly update him or her on the amount of time remaining. If you're running the study remotely using a videoconferencing solution, make sure audio/video is working correctly. If you're running an in-person lab study, make sure the equipment is working properly.

OBSERVER: Find a location where you can observe the customer. You should consider putting away all devices, including laptops and cell phones. Remove any distractions that might get in the way of observing the customer. If you want to take notes, consider taking them with pen and paper to avoid the temptation of checking messages or responding to email.

2. MAKE THE INTRODUCTIONS (APPROXIMATELY 5 MINUTES).
MODERATOR:

1. Begin the introduction by welcoming the customer and thanking them for their willingness to participate in the study.

2. Introduce yourself and anyone from the team who has joined the study.

3. Briefly describe the objectives of the study.

4. Encourage the customer to be open and honest in their feedback. There are no right or wrong answers. You're testing the product, not the customer. Any information they provide will help you and the team learn. Even if their comments are negative, it will not hurt your feelings; it will only help you and the team develop better products. Remind them that it's important for them to tell you if they're confused or frustrated by anything they experience during the study.

5. Ask for permission to record the session.

NOTE TAKER: Record the date, time, and the team members that are participating in the study.

TIMEKEEPER/COORDINATOR: Once the study begins, start the clock and begin tracking the time.

3. BREAK THE ICE (APPROXIMATELY 10 MINUTES).
MODERATOR:

- Use the Discussion Guide to steer the conversation, including the questions about the [type of customers], [problem], and [job-to-be-done]. At this point in the study, you're only getting to know the customer. They haven't begun to interact with the prototype.

- Try to keep the tone conversational, rather than reading off a script. This will become easier and more natural the more practice you have.

NOTE TAKER: Continue to capture as much as the customer says. You can use the Discussion Guide as a template for your responses. As best you can, don't paraphrase.

TIMEKEEPER/COORDINATOR: Signify to the moderator when they have reached a milestone (e.g., "10 minutes left," "5 minutes left," "1 more minute"). You can do this by writing on a notepad, sending a private IM, or passing a Post-it note.

4. CONDUCT THE TASK-BASED PORTION OF THE STUDY (APPROXIMATELY 40–70 MINUTES).

MODERATOR:

- At this point you'll present the prototype and provide the customer with written or verbal instructions on the tasks you'd like them to perform. It's important that you are not *demonstrating* the feature. Give customers just enough instruction so they know what they need to do. Your instructions should *not* include how to do it.

- Remind the customer to think out loud as they walk through the tasks and describe what they are doing and why.

- Resist the urge to help the customer complete the task. Learn first, then help. You want to get to the root cause and thoroughly understand what they're struggling with and why.

- If the customer is spending an excess amount of time on a task, you can encourage them to move on to the next task.

- Remember to ask probing and clarifying questions when necessary.

- Pay close attention to the customer's physical reactions. They may be communicating a positive sentiment, but their facial expression or body language is expressing frustration or confusion.

NOTE TAKER: As best you can, try to:

- Capture anything the customer says.

- Document success or failure.

- Take note of physical reactions such as body language or facial expressions.

- Document any situations where the customer tries to complete the task in an unexpected way.

- Capture any discrepancies between how the customer verbally responds and what you observed (e.g., they say, "This works great!" even though they struggled to complete the task).

TIMEKEEPER/COORDINATOR: Signify to the moderator when they have reached a milestone (e.g., "10 minutes left," "5 minutes left," "1 more minute). You can do this by writing on a notepad, sending a private IM, or passing a Post-it note.

5. WRAP UP (APPROXIMATELY 5 MINUTES).

MODERATOR:

1. Use this time to bring the study to an end. Ask any clarifying questions if necessary.

2. Open the call up to the team, allowing them to ask questions.

3. Answer any questions the customer may have. If they request help with a task they struggled with, this would be a good time to discuss it or provide help. Remind them that, if they struggled with it, other customers will too and that it's something the team will need to address.

4. Thank the customer for their time and feedback.

5. Provide gratuity for their time.

6. Ask for referrals—anyone they would recommend who would want to talk to you.

NOTE TAKER:

1. Review your notes and determine if you need any more detail. When the moderator opens the call, ask the customer any questions that can help clarify what you captured.

2. When the notes are complete, be sure to include them in the team's shoebox.

TIMEKEEPER:

1. Stop the recording.

2. Keep the recording in your shoebox or another shared location.

Debriefing After Usability Studies

It's important to allocate time with the team, shortly after the usability test, to give everyone a chance to share their insights and make suggestions for updates or iterations necessary for the next study.

Sensemaking

Schematizing the Data

Once the team has completed a series of usability tests, it's time to interpret the customers' feedback.

1. LABEL YOUR TASKS WITH AN ID.

1. For each task, write it on a large Post-it note.

2. In the upper-left corner, write a unique number or ID.

3. Hang each task on the wall or board horizontally, so that you can create columns for each task (see Figure 13-3).

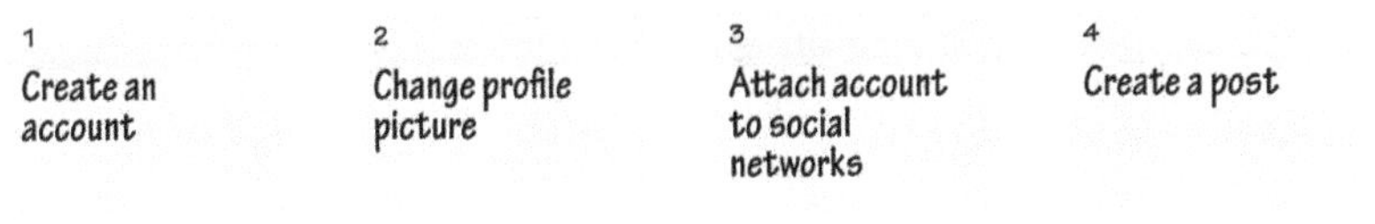

1	2	3	4
Create an account	Change profile picture	Attach account to social networks	Create a post

FIGURE 13-3
Large Post-it notes are hung on the wall and laid out horizontally to create columns for each task

2. TAG THE CUSTOMERS' FEEDBACK.

For each task:

1. Watch the video and review your notes.

2. When you discover or observe something meaningful, write it down on a Post-it note. In the upper-left corner, tag it with the task ID.

3. In the upper-right of the note, tag it with the reason you found it meaningful (see Figure 13-4).

4. Hang the Post-it note under the appropriate task.

3   **C**

Couldn't locate button to attach Twitter account. Didn't think Twitter was supported.

FIGURE 13-4
Post-it note documenting a situation where the customer was confused during a task

TABLE 13-1. Lists some tags you could use.

TAG	TYPE OF FEEDBACK
Validate/**I**nvalidate	Comments that validate or invalidate your Feature hypotheses
Satisfaction/**D**issatisfaction	Comments that suggest customers were satisfied or dissatisfied with the feature
Useful	Comments that indicate that the feature is (or is not) useful or valuable
Solves a **P**roblem	Statements that suggest the feature is (or is not) solving a problem for the customer
Frustration	Behaviors or comments that indicate the customer was frustrated
Error	Situations where the customer encountered an unexpected error
Confusion	Behaviors or comments that suggest the customer was confused or lost while trying to complete the task

3. IDENTIFY PATTERNS OF SUCCESS AND IMPROVEMENT.

Look at the notes hung under each task and identify patterns of confusion, frustration, or success.

On the large Post-it note where you wrote the task, label it with the following:

Pivot

A task shows a cluster of Post-it notes where customers could not discover the feature, were unsuccessful, or found the interaction unsatisfactory.

Needs iterations

There are patterns of Post-it notes that suggest customers struggled but were ultimately successful with the interaction and were at least somewhat satisfied.

Success

Customers were successful and satisfied or very satisfied with the task, and thus no changes are necessary.

4. ASSESS THE ENTIRETY OF THE EXPERIENCE.

While it's important to understand what features and interactions have landed with the customer, it's also important to consider the *entire flow* of the experience. Look at all your tasks as representative of the success of your overall MVP and ask yourself:

- Are there major points in the workflow that are creating friction points for the customer? What are they?

- What parts of the overall experience are working well? Can we replicate those experiences in other places where the flow is more problematic?

- Are customers using the collection of features in a way that was anticipated?

- Are we confident that this collection of features (the MVP) is delivering on what customers found valuable during the Concept stage?

- What's our level of confidence that, if we shipped the MVP today with the features designed as they are now, it would be successful with customers? What else do we need to know to raise our level of confidence?

Updating the Evidence File

Now that your team has spent time schematizing the data, update your evidence file. It should contain the most meaningful bits of data that comprise the team's point of view, vision, and product strategy, including:

[NOTE]
For more information on the evidence file, see Chapter 4.

- Validated and invalidated hypotheses

- Quotes that exemplify success, desire, frustration, or failure

- Documentation supporting the reasons you'll be pivoting, making iterations, or continuing with the design

- Your assessment of the overall design and flow of the entire experience

- Any next steps that will raise confidence that the features will deliver on the benefits that customers found valuable during the Concept stage

Creating and Sharing Your Stories

As customer advocates, share the information you've learned with your organization using the channels you've established as a team (stand-ups, email alias, presentations, or newsletters).

Consider communicating:

- The validated and invalidated Feature hypotheses

- Video clips showing the customer's reaction to the feature

- A spider diagram highlighting how strongly each design iteration met the principles identified during the Concept stage (see Figure 13-5)

- The organization of features into actionable categories (e.g., Pivot, Needs Iterations, Success)

- Design recommendations that help deliver on the principles established during the Concept stage

- The changes the team made to the feature design and connecting those decisions with direct customer feedback

FIGURE 13-5
This spider diagram illustrates how various feature designs performed against the concept's principles

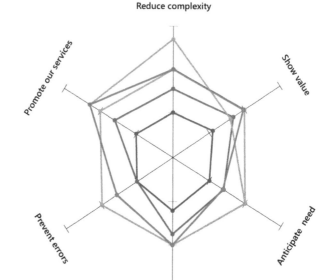

SHARE THE STORY

You've established multiple lines of communication with your organization to share your learnings. You've completed the Feature stage and you're confident that you have a product customers will love, but that doesn't mean you're finished. Remember that your customers are a moving target, so as they continue to grow and learn, you'll want to anticipate their needs and look for areas of opportunity. Continue to stay engaged with customers and share your learnings with your organization.

[*Afterword*]

If you're looking for additional materials for you or your team, head over to *customerdrivenplaybook.com* for more activities and templates. We encourage to make these practices your own. If an activity doesn't quite align for you and your team, make changes to it so that it does (and be sure to share it with us!).

At the end of the day, the customer-driven strategy is successful because it keeps the customer at the center of your decision-making. It's successful because it creates a sustaining feedback loop. Look for ways to continually engage with your customers, collect their feedback, and internalize what they're saying. Bring them into your process and leverage their unique perspectives to gain insights and drive your product's strategy.

Finally, we'd like to say thanks for taking the time to read our book. As far as we're concerned, you're *our* customer. So feel free to connect with us over Twitter (*@tlowdermilk* and *@JessRichPhD*). We'd love to hear from you and answer any questions you might have.

[*References*]

[99pi] Mars, Roman. "99 Percent Invisible." On Average. Published August 23, 2016. *http://99percentinvisible.org/episode/on-average/*.

[AEIOU] EthnoHub. "AEIOU Framework." Accessed March 8, 2017. *http://help.ethnohub.com/guide/aeiou-framework*.

[alvarez] Alvarez, Cindy. *Lean Customer Development: Build Products Your Customers Will Buy*. Sebastopol, CA: O'Reilly Media, 2014. ISBN: 978-1-4493-5635-4.

[anderson] Anderson, Peggy. *Great Quotes from Great Leaders: Words from the Leaders Who Shaped the World*. Naperville, IL: Simple Truths, 2017. ISBN: 978-1-4926-4961-8.

[atwood] Atwood, Jeff. "The Pontiac Aztek and the Perils of Design by Committee." Coding Horror: Programming and Human Factors, June 16, 2005. *https://blog.codinghorror.com/the-pontiac-aztek-and-the-perils-of-design-by-committee/*.

[basadur] "Reducing Complexity in Conceptual Thinking Using Challenge Mapping." ResearchGate, January 1, 2003. *https://www.researchgate.net/publication/228542745_Reducing_Complexity_in_Conceptual_Thinking_Using_Challenge_Mapping*.

[basadur-innovation] Basadur, Min. *The Power of Innovation: How to Make Innovation a Way of Life and Put Creative Solutions to Work*. Burlington, ON: Applied Creativity Press, 2001. ISBN: 0-273-61362-6.

[beren] Beren, David. "T-Mobile Announces Fourth Quarter 2011 Financial Results, LTE Network Coming In 2013." Accessed February 20, 2017. *http://www.tmonews.com/2012/02/t-mobile-announces-fourth-quarter-2011-financial-results-lte-network-coming-in-2013/*.

[christensen] Christensen, Clayton M., Karen Dillon, Taddy Hall, and David S. Duncan. *Competing Against Luck: The Story of Innovation and Customer Choice*. New York: HarperBusiness, 2016.

[continuum] Continuum Innovation. Case Studies: Swiffer. Accessed December 20, 2016. *https://www.continuuminnovation.com/en/what-we-do/case-studies/swiffer*.

[daniels] Daniels, Gilbert S. "The 'Average Man'?" Air Force Aerospace Medical Research Lab, Wright-Patterson AFB OH, December 1952.

[epstein] Epstein, Zach. "T-Mobile Grows Branded Subscriber Base for First Time in Four Years in Q1." BGR, April 4, 2013. *http://bgr.com/2013/04/04/t-mobile-earnings-q1-2013-414479/*.

[flint] Flint, Jerry. "The Pontiac Aztek: GM Stumbles Again." *Forbes*, January 26, 2001. *http://www.forbes.com/2001/01/26/0126flint.html*.

[glass] Glass, Sandie. "What Were They Thinking? The Day Ketchup Crossed the Line from Perfect to Purple." Fast Company, September 14, 2011. *http://www.fastcompany.com/1779591/what-were-they-thinking-day-ketchup-crossed-line-perfect-purple*.

[goodman] Goodman, Elizabeth, Mike Kuniavsky, and Andrea Moed. *Observing the User Experience: A Practitioner's Guide to User Research*, 2nd ed. Amsterdam, Boston: Morgan Kaufmann, 2012.

[gothelf] Gothelf, Jeff and Josh Seiden. *Lean UX: Designing Great Products with Agile Teams*, 2nd ed. Sebastopol, CA: O'Reilly Media, 2016.

[gray] Gray, Dave, Sunni Brown, and James Macanufo. *Gamestorming: A Playbook for Innovators, Rulebreakers, and Changemakers*. Sebastopol, CA: O'Reilly Media, 2010.

[greve] Greve, Frank. "Ketchup Is Better with Upside-Down, Bigger Bottle." McClatchy Newspapers, June 28, 2007. *http://www.mcclatchydc.com/news/nation-world/national/article24465613.html*.

[heinz-commercial] "Matt Le Blanc - Heinz Ketchup Commercial." Accessed January 24, 2017. YouTube.

[howe] Howe, Tom. "Sony's First U.S. Betamax Product, the TV/VCR Combo LV-1901 from 1975." Accessed January 19, 2017. *http://www.cedmagic.com/history/betamax-lv-1901.html*.

[humble] Humble, Jez, Joanne Molesky, and Barry O'Reilly. *Lean Enterprise*. Sebastopol, CA: O'Reilly Media, 2014.

[janis] Janis, Irving Lester. *Groupthink: Psychological Studies of Policy Decisions and Fiascoes*, 2nd ed. Boston: Houghton Mifflin, 1983.

[janis-political-psychology] Hart, Paul't. "Irving L. Janis's Victims of Groupthink." *Political Psychology* vol. 12, no. 2 (June 1991), pp. 247–278. International Society of Political Psychology.

[kelley] Kelley, Tom and David Kelley. *Creative Confidence: Unleashing the Creative Potential Within Us All*. New York: Crown Business, 2013.

[lafley] Lafley, A. G. and Roger L. Martin. *Playing to Win: How Strategy Really Works*. Boston: Harvard Business Review Press, 2013.

[lund] Lund, Arnold. "Measuring Usability with the USE Questionnaire." ResearchGate. Accessed April 14, 2017. *https://www.researchgate.net/publication/230786746_Measuring_usability_with_the_USE_questionnaire*.

[lutz] Lutz, Bob. "Complete Acquiescence: Bob Lutz Reveals How the Pontiac Aztek Happened [UPDATE: Our Own Don Sherman Responds]." *Car and Driver* blog, October 14, 2014. *http://blog.caranddriver.com/complete-acquiesence-bob-lutz-reveals-how-the-pontiac-aztek-happened/*.

[maurya] Maurya, Ash. *Running Lean: Iterate from Plan A to a Plan That Works*, 2nd ed. Sebastopol, CA: O'Reilly Media, 2012.

[meola] Meola, Andrew. "T-Mobile refuses to go away in the wireless carrier war," *Business Insider*. Accessed February 21, 2017. *http://www.businessinsider.com/t-mobile-continues-growth-against-verizon-sprint-att-2016-4*.

[miller] Miller, Joe. "Pontiac's Aztek Aims for Young, Hip." Automotive News 74, no. 5857 (January 17, 2000).

[moore] Moore, David T. *Sensemaking: A Structure for An Intelligence Revolution*, 2nd ed. CreateSpace Independent Publishing Platform, 2013.

[mozart] Mozart, Mike. "Heinz Ketchup." April 30, 2016. *https://www.flickr.com/photos/jeepersmedia/26135496253/*.

[petroski] Petroski, Henry. "ASK OCE Interview: Five Questions for Dr. Henry Petroski | APPEL – Academy of Program/Project & Engineering Leadership." Accessed April 13, 2017. *https://appel.nasa. gov/2010/02/26/ao_1-10_f_interview-html/.*

[pirolli] Pirolli, Peter and Stuart Card. "The Sensemaking Process and Leverage Points for Analyst Technology as Identified Through Cognitive Task Analysis." In *Proceedings of International Conference on Intelligence Analysis,* vol. 5 (2005), pp. 2–4.

[ries] Ries, Eric. *The Lean Startup: How Today's Entrepreneurs Use Continuous Innovation to Create Radically Successful Businesses.* New York: Crown Business, 2011.

[roca] Roca, Carrie. "Pontiac Aztek: GM's First Crossover Is Onboard to Make a Splash." *Autoweek,* June 11, 2000. *http://autoweek.com/article/ car-news/pontiac-aztek-gms-first-crossover-onboard-make-splash.*

[rose] Rose, Todd. "When U.S. Air Force Discovered the Flaw of Averages." TheStar.com. January 16, 2016. *https://www.thestar.com/ news/insight/2016/01/16/when-us-air-force-discovered-the-flaw-of-averages.html.*

[seabaugh] Seabaugh, Christian. "GM Designer Tom Peters on Camaro, Corvette, and Pontiac Aztek." *Motor Trend,* April 26, 2014. *http://www. motortrend.com/news/gm-designer-tom-peters-on-camaro-corvette -and-pontiac-aztek/.*

[sony] "Sony Promotional Video for the VERY FIRST Betamax—1975!!" Accessed January 19, 2017. *http://www.youtube.com/watch?v=Lt2KlIEr5xA.*

[un-carrier] "T-Mobile's Un-Carrier Event | T-Mobile Newsroom." Accessed February 20, 2017. *https://newsroom.t-mobile.com/media-kits/t-mobiles-un-carrier-event.htm.*

[video] "Videotape Format War." Wikipedia, January 6, 2017. *https:// en.wikipedia.org/w/index.php?title=Videotape_format_war&oldid= 758683779.*

[weisman] Weisman, Jonathan. "Biggest Automaker Needs Big Changes." *Washington Post,* June 11, 2005, *http://www.washingtonpost .com/wp-dyn/content/article/2005/06/10/AR2005061002188.html.*

[wielage] Wielage, Marc and Rod Woodcock. "The Rise and Fall of Beta." Videofax. 1988. *http://www.betainfoguide.net/RiseandFall.htm.*

[Index]

A

A/B testing, 36
achievable (task criteria), 113, 204
administering surveys, 34
Air Force cockpit size example, 79–81
Alvarez, Cindy, 33, 44, 58, 74
analogies in storytelling, 52
analytics
  about, 36
  advantages, 36
  disadvantages, 36–37
  schematizing data from customer visits, 142–145
  schematizing data from CVT, 192–194
  schematizing data from interviews, 163–166
  schematizing data from usability studies, 215–217
  survey tools, 35
assumptions
  formulating, 9
  formulating for Customer playbook, 126–128
  formulating for Problem playbook, 150–152
  formulating into hypotheses, 15–16
  Gillette razor example, 67–68
  Pontiac Aztek example, 5–6
  testing, 19–20
"average man", 79–81

B

Basadur, Min, 83–85
behaviors, separating persons from, 22–23
Bergh, Chip, 67
Betamax example, 91–93
blitzing activity, 84
Brown, Paul, 108
Build action. *See* Formulating action (CDC)
business goals, prioritizing ideas based on, 86

C

Card, Stuart, 47
causation and correlation, 14
Christensen, Clayton, 17
churners, 22–23
concept (HPF parameter), 88, 175–176, 183
Concept playbook
  about, 169–170
  concept parameter, 175–176, 183
  conducting Concept Value Test, 187–191
  creating and sharing stories, 196–197
  criteria parameter, 176–177
  debriefing after Concept Value Test, 191–192
  determining must have benefits, 194–195
  formulate concept benefits, 177–178
  formulate concept limitations, 178–179
  formulating Discussion Guide, 182–184
  formulating ideas, 170–173
  formulating unique value proposition, 177
  job-to-be-done parameter, 182
  plotting events using storyboards, 179–182
  preparing for Concept Value Test, 184–186
  prioritizing ideas using Impact/Effort Matrix, 173–175
  problem parameter, 170–172, 183
  schematizing the data, 192–194
  turning ideas into concepts, 175–177
  type of customer parameter, 182
  updating evidence file, 196
Concept stage (HPF)
  Air Force cockpit size example, 79–81
  concept parameter, 88
  Concept Value Test, 94–101
  criteria parameter, 88
  formulating hypotheses, 87–88
  formulating ideas, 82–85
  fundamental questions in, 8–9, 81, 83–85, 94–95, 97–99
  job-to-be-done parameter, 88
  picking best potential opportunity, 85–87
  plotting events using storyboards, 90–91

fundamental in Problem stage, 7, 75
"How might we?", 83–85, 170–173
icebreaker, 137–138, 188–189
magic wand, 74
open-ended, 26
screening for interviews, 30, 157
USE questionnaire, 111
"Quick Wins" (Impact/Effort Matrix), 86–87, 173–174, 201

R

ratings (CVT), 96–99, 189, 192
reasonable (task criteria), 113, 204
red flag responses, 98, 193
"Reducing Complexity in Conceptual Thinking" (Basadur), 83–85
relationships, establishing with customers, 43
Ries, Eric, 9
risk
    prioritizing ideas based on, 85
    reducing with hypotheses, 20, 33
roles
    during Concept Value Test, 186–191
    during customer visits, 134–141
    during interview process, 31–32, 158–161
    during usability studies, 209–214

S

sample size
    for analytics, 36
    for CVT, 96
    for interviews, 33–34
    for surveys, 34
schedules
    preparing for Concept Value Test, 185–186
    preparing for interviews, 157–158
    preparing for usability studies, 208–209
schemas (sensemaking loop)
    about, 48, 51
    schematic data from customer visits, 142–145
    schematizing data from CVT, 192–194
    schematizing data from interviews, 163–166
    schematizing data from usability studies, 215–217
screeners
    for Concept Value Test, 184
    for interview process, 30, 157
    for usability studies, 208

Sensemaking action (CDC)
    about, 10, 47
    in Concept playbook, 192–197
    in Customer playbook, 142–148
    in Feature playbook, 215–219
    in Problem playbook, 163–168
    sensemaking loop, 47–53
sensemaking loop
    about, 47–49
    data sources, 48–49
    evidence file, 48, 50–51, 146, 167, 196, 217
    schemas, 48, 51, 142–145, 163–166, 192–194, 215–217
    shoeboxes, 48, 50, 132, 152, 173
    stories, 48, 52–53, 146–148, 167–168, 196–197, 218–219
sequential (task criteria), 113, 205
shared parameters (HPF), 16–19
shoeboxes (sensemaking loop)
    about, 48, 50
    for Concept playbook, 173
    for Customer playbook, 132
    for Problem playbook, 152
Sievert, Mike, 56
sketches (prototypes), 205
skill, as a customer limitation, 70
social networks
    for finding customers, 41
    getting customer's attention via, 42–43
"soft" quantitative data, 25–26, 96–99
Sony Betamax example, 91–93
specific (criteria)
    for hypotheses, 20–22
    for tasks, 113, 205
spider diagrams, 218
StarDoc tool, 58–61, 73–74
stories (sensemaking loop)
    about, 48, 52–53
    creating and sharing from customer visits, 146–148
    creating and sharing from CVT, 196–197
    creating and sharing from interviews, 167–168
    creating and sharing from usability studies, 218–219
storyboards
    plotting event using, 90–91, 179–182
    presenting during CVT, 188
surveys
    advantages of, 34–35
    disadvantages of, 35–36
Swiffer Sweeper example, 70–71

[About the Authors]

Travis Lowdermilk, author of *User-Centered Design: A Developer's Guide to Building User Friendly Applications,* has been building software experiences as both a developer and a designer for over 15 years. Currently, Travis is a UX Designer at Microsoft, helping teams apply design thinking and Lean principles to their products.

To learn more about Travis, visit *travislowdermilk.com* or follow him on Twitter (*@tlowdermilk*).

Dr. Jessica Rich is a UX Researcher at Microsoft with a PhD in Human Factors. With over a decade of experience in the software industry, Jessica has led teams through customer and product development using Lean strategies.